Simon & Schuster

New York   London   Toronto   Sydney   New Delhi

At Home with
MADAME CHIC

Becoming a Connoisseur
of
Daily Life

JENNIFER L. SCOTT

Simon & Schuster
1230 Avenue of the Americas
New York, NY 10020

First Simon & Schuster hardcover edition October 2014

SIMON & SCHUSTER and colophon are registered trademarks of Simon & Schuster, Inc.

For information about special discounts for bulk purchases, please contact Simon & Schuster Special Sales at 1-866-506-1949 or business@simonandschuster.com.

The Simon & Schuster Speakers Bureau can bring authors to your live event. For more information or to book an event contact the Simon & Schuster Speakers Bureau at 1-866-248-3049 or visit our website at www.simonspeakers.com.

Jacket design by Jackie Seow
Jacket and text illustrations by Virginia Johnson/Illustration Division

Manufactured in the United States of America

10 9 8 7 6 5 4 3 2 1

Library of Congress Cataloging-in-Publication Data
Scott, Jennifer L. (Jennifer Lynn)
    At home with Madame Chic : becoming a connoisseur of daily life /
Jennifer L. Scott.
        pages cm
    1. Charm. 2. Fashion. 3. Home economics. 4. Women—France—Paris—Social life and customs. 5. French—Social life and customs. 6. Self-help / Motivational & Inspirational. 7. House & home / Cleaning & Caretaking. 8. Paris (France)—Social life and customs. 9. Paris (France)—Civilization. I. Title.
    BJ1610 .S3947 2014
    646.7   2014015011

ISBN 978-1-4767-7033-8
ISBN 978-1-4767-7034-5 (ebook)

For Gary and Sonia Evans

Contents

At Home with

MADAME
CHIC

INTRODUCTION

◟ What Is Chic? ◞

What is chic? Chic is a feeling. It's a state of mind. It is a way to live and a way to be. We've all seen chic people. Nicely dressed, they seem to have a strong understanding of what their true style is. But it's so much more than their clothing, isn't it? Chic people have an air of mystery about them. They seem content with something, but what that is . . . we can't put our finger on it. Their chicness appears effortless, as though the graceful way they get through the day comes naturally to them.

When looking at these chic people, you might wonder if they have a cluttered living room, or if they scramble to figure out what to have for dinner at six p.m. every evening. You wonder if they detest emptying the dishwasher as much as you do. Heck, look at that manicure. Do these chic people even do the dishes?

Well, some of them probably don't. But what about the rest of us? Being chic has nothing to do with money. Not all chic people are rich, and not all rich people are chic. You may have observed this with reality television. You might see a wealthy woman with the perfect haircut, dressed in the latest designer clothes. She has a big house, a sports car, and that magic wand, fame. But her negative attitude, insecurities, and bad manners combine to make her, as they say, a hot mess. This type of person does not possess that chic *je ne sais quoi*. She has a lot of inner work to do.

Being chic is not about the size of your bank account. It has nothing to do with where you live. It has nothing to do with the job you have or the person you're married to. It has nothing to do with the car you drive or the labels on your clothes. Chic is a state of being. And it is something that anyone can cultivate. Yes, anyone.

You can be chic. You can have a beautiful, productive, and passionate life. You can flow gracefully through your day and look good while doing it. You can find happiness in your life, even if everything isn't exactly how you pictured it would be. If you are used to a chaotic, unorganized, and so-not-chic life, don't fret. That doesn't have to be your reality.

In my first book, *Lessons from Madame Chic: 20 Stylish Secrets I Learned While Living in Paris*, I introduced Madame Chic and her fabulous Parisian family. The secrets of fine living I learned from Famille Chic planted the seeds of inspiration in my life and opened up a whole new world for me. After those blissful, carefree days as a student in Paris, I moved back to America and eventually found myself with my own home and family to look after. I wanted to espouse the elegant way of living I learned in Paris and become my own version of Madame Chic. But back home in California, everyday life was no longer idyllic; it was *messy*. What would Madame Chic say if she could see my bedroom, our living room, or the backseat of my car? Without my mentor to guide me, I had to rely on myself to get to the core of what it means to live well when you have a family, a home, and a busy life. And let me tell you, it wasn't chic.

You may think that being chic has nothing to do with the most insignificant and mundane moments of the day. Moments like preparing your meals, emptying the dishwasher, and paying bills. But the secret is: those moments aren't insignificant. *Au contraire.* They are very significant. That's right—if you can change your attitude about making the pasta sauce, choosing your clothes for the day, folding the laundry, setting the table, or dealing with the incoming mail, you can completely change your life. I'm going to show you how you can derive pleasure from these seemingly mundane tasks, how you can turn all that frustrated and chaotic energy into satisfied, pleasurable energy. After you form an initial organization plan and a routine that becomes second nature, your home will run more smoothly, and you will learn to enjoy and enhance your routine. This peace will follow you wherever you go for the rest of the day, no matter how far you venture from home.

Your home is a microcosm of the real world. The more you practice living well at home, the more natural it will feel to carry this practice out into the real world, and the closer you'll be to becoming your own Madame Chic. If you have a home life that runs smoothly, you too will have that air of effortlessness about you. You'll spend less negative energy worrying about where you put your keys, or what you're going to have for dinner, or how on earth you're going to clean up the mess in the living room.

Your attitude will shift. There will be something about you—something mysterious that other people can't quite figure out. That *je ne sais quoi* quality *is* chic.

What Is *Je ne Sais Quoi?*

Je ne sais quoi: that "certain something." This is a phrase we've all heard. It describes people who just have "it." But what is "it"? And how can we get it? Is *je ne sais quoi* being skinny? Is it having perfect highlights in your hair? Can you buy *je ne sais quoi*? What if I buy this season's hottest clothes? Does that give me *je ne sais quoi*? The answer to all of these questions is *non*. That's because *je ne sais quoi* is intangible. It is not something on the outside; it is something within. In *A Return to Love*, Marianne Williamson describes charisma as "a sparkle in people that money can't buy. It's an invisible energy with visible effects."

That charisma she's talking about is a part of *je ne sais quoi*. It's that sparkle—that magnetism—that fuels one's air of mystery.

Here is another secret no one tells you: that *je ne sais quoi* comes from inner peace. It is having inner peace while you are drying the pots and pans. It is having inner peace while you choose your outfit for the day or while you walk the dog. It is having inner peace when you are in the midst of a difficult conversation, meeting a deadline in the office, lugging the groceries up the stairs, or even sitting in traffic at five p.m. Chic people have that *je ne sais quoi*, and that "certain something" is inner peace.

Having inner peace should always be our goal. Then we can get through our day no matter what happens around us. Once we have it, small things, such as a careless comment from a coworker or a flat tire, will not completely ruin our day. Inner peace will keep us present and put things into perspective. People will wonder how you manage to navigate through life so gracefully. They will wonder about that "certain something" about you that they can't quite put their finger on. Your inner peace will be intriguing and will draw people to you.

But how on earth does one cultivate inner peace when the pasta is boiling over, the baby is teething, the toddler is having a tantrum, and the dog just peed on the curtains? Really, you have no other choice but chic. You can wallow in anger and despair, but where does that really get you in the end? Or you can remain calm. You can breathe. You can deal with one thing at a time and not let anything, no matter how loud or pressing, fill you with anxiety. If this seems impossible, let's examine another phrase often used to describe chic people.

～ What Is *Bien dans Sa Peau?* ～

Bien dans sa peau translates as "comfortable in her skin." People who are *bien dans leur peau* do not have inner turmoil and constant neuroses ruling their lives. They are not always worrying if they've said or done the right thing. They aren't constantly trying to please people and be everything to everybody. They are comfortable being who they are. They enjoy themselves. They value themselves. This too is inner peace.

Instead of opening your closet and going through a neurotic dialogue about how you need to lose fifteen pounds before you look good in any of your clothes, you are *bien dans ta peau.* You know you are beautiful right now, so you pick a beautiful outfit and wear it. If you are *bien dans ta peau*, doing the dishes is not annoying and beneath you. It is important and valuable work. You enjoy the process. If you are *bien dans ta peau*, your financial life is important, so you pay your bills on time and file away the receipts (and you don't rack yourself with financial worries during the process). If you are *bien dans ta peau*, you can remain calm when you have a disagreement with your spouse. If *je ne sais quoi* is inner peace, then *bien dans sa peau* is putting inner peace first. Now we can finally define that elusive quality of chic. But how do you get it? To start you need two things: curiosity and enthusiasm. And then you need to become a connoisseur of your own life.

What Is a Connoisseur?

The dictionary defines a connoisseur as an "expert judge in matters of taste." One can be a connoisseur of music, for example, or wine. I like to think of myself as a connoisseur of life. I first heard the phrase in a lesser-known Agatha Christie short story collection called *The Mysterious Mr. Quin*. The main character, Mr. Satterthwaite, is described as a connoisseur. He cultivates fine taste in everything from his food to his clothing. He is also an ardent observer of others and gets a kick out of determining what makes people tick. This was where I got the inspiration to name my blog *The Daily Connoisseur*. If one can become an aficionado in all things wine and appreciate and savor the different varieties, for example, why not apply that philosophy to everything we do in a day?

Being a Madame Chic goes hand in hand with becoming a connoisseur of your own life. Having passion and appreciation for the ordinary. Getting a kick out of everything you do. It is looking at everyday life like a sporting challenge and doing whatever it takes to make it work for you. Enthusiasm is the key that unlocks the chic in everyday life. We will become connoisseurs of our home life. We will apply this sporting attitude, this curiosity, this *verve* to rising in the morning, going to bed at night, and to everything that happens in between.

Are You for Real?

On your quest to become your own Madame Chic, you decide to do some research. You pick up some books about style and beauty. You read these books and try to tie your scarf a certain way or eat a certain thing for breakfast or buy the wardrobe investment pieces. You might get a makeover and color your hair and find the right shade of lipstick to complement your scarf. All of this can be fun. And, yes, you might look darn good. But are you completely satisfied? Are you chic?

Okay, then maybe you need to get your home life in order. There's no point in looking chic if your home is a complete disaster. You read design books and decide on your own interior design aesthetic. You go shopping and update your furniture. You paint the walls. You will look chic and live in a chic home. But something is missing. Now your beautiful, newly decorated home is getting trashed by the kids every afternoon and you start to feel helpless. Your husband is annoying you because he just doesn't get why it's important that the throw pillows stay on the sofa. You feel overwhelmed because you have to figure out what's for dinner, and at the end of the day you are so tired that you don't even want to think about cleaning up your now not-so-chic house. Or self.

You feel completely lost in a sea of hopelessness. One afternoon you have a half hour off, so you go buy a new lipstick or a pair of shoes, hoping that it will make you feel better. It temporarily feels good, but the buzz doesn't last for long. You feel so unfulfilled at home. You see your friends on Facebook with their high-powered careers and exciting dating lives, and then you think about the messy home all around you. You didn't sign up for this. Cleaning all day long? Constantly negotiating with your kids? Arguing with your husband? You wish you could transplant yourself to Paris, just for an afternoon, where you could be someone else. You could be that chic woman sitting at a café, serenely enjoying life.

But right now that isn't a reality. You start to feel angry. You've done everything they said it would take! You have given yourself a makeover. You have the hottest handbag. You have perfect highlights in your hair. You bought those new throw pillows for your sofa that promised to add a pop of color to your living room. So what's the problem? Why don't you feel chic?

Then you start to think maybe the problem stems from the inside. So you pick up a lot of self-help books. The advice in these books blows you away. You start to read about being present, about not being a people pleaser, about not taking things personally. You start to learn about meditation, inner peace, gratitude, and the law of attraction. You are attracted to all of it. When you are reading the books, it all makes so much sense. But then you put the books down and it all goes out of your head. How can you keep the faith when you are trying to get your kids to help with cleanup time and they're not listening to you (again!)? How can you remain in the present moment when you would rather be anywhere but in your laundry room folding towels? You know you should practice gratitude daily, but sometimes it feels hard, especially when you feel like your family is bursting out of your tiny house and you can't afford to move to a bigger place.

Gosh, there's so much to work on. You start to wonder how things like lip gloss and scarves are even relevant when you are trying to cultivate inner peace. Is style even important? You're not going to be a people pleaser anymore, right? So why do you need to dress up to impress people? You know you need to get rid of your clutter (you read a feng shui book) but how can you begin to tackle that problem without being stopped by a feeling of dread? Is it possible to get through a day without detesting a large percentage of the things you have to do?

If you haven't already guessed, I am writing about myself.

These are the questions I posed to myself on so many occasions. But I am also hazarding a bet that you can relate to much of what I say. The style books give you lots of ideas on beauty and fashion. The home books tell you how to get your house organized and decorate. The self-help books give you advice on how to meditate and clear your inner turmoil. But how on earth does the stay-at-home mom of three children or the woman with nine-hour workdays and a long commute incorporate these ideas into her real, messy, everyday life? How does she make these concepts work for her? How does she work on herself from the inside, look beautiful on the outside, and navigate through the long day ahead of cleaning, working, parenting, and cooking without losing herself in the process? How can she not only "get through it," but *thrive in it*?

This book will bridge the gap for you. Seemingly superficial topics, such as choosing your clothes for the day, will be discussed, along with deeper topics like inner peace and mindfulness. Meditation will be discussed right along with clutter-busting tips. Because it all goes together. This is life, and we must not only live it but celebrate it. *All of it*. It's okay to get excited about trying a new cake recipe and bringing out your best tablecloth. It's okay to care how you look every day and to adorn yourself beautifully. Because all of this is a celebration of life. The more aware we become, the more inner peace we cultivate, the more present we are, the more we are able to enjoy every moment of life. We begin to live life how we were meant to live: with celebration, love, and devotion behind everything we do. Finding the divine in every aspect of our day starts at home. So, yes, tips on getting your family to sit down for dinner can exist on the same page with exercises to cultivate inner peace, because, you see, it all goes hand in hand.

Madame Chic Reincarnated

When I lived with Madame Chic in Paris, I was always impressed with how she looked so put together every day. Nothing about her appearance seemed high maintenance. Her style was inherent, from her dark-brown Parisian bob to her A-line skirts to her low-heeled pumps. There were no off days when she ran around the house in sweatpants with unkempt hair. Every day for her was a meditation in beauty—from the way she put together an outfit to the way she cooked dinner. I got the impression that she had always been that way. Who knows whether that was true, but she was so comfortable in her own skin and in her own routine that her elegance appeared effortless.

As we know, Madame Chic was a master at cultivating her air of mystery. She just did what she did without explaining it (and looked pretty darn happy while doing it!). And as a naïve college student living with her, I wasn't exactly paying attention to how she ran her home so stylishly. Back then I was more interested in what Parisian hot spots my friends and I would hit up next. So you can see why, a decade later, I would be jogging my memory trying to figure out how she did all of it.

I remembered that she woke up before the entire family to prepare breakfast. She did the washing on the same days each week and had cleaning systems she rarely deviated from. I know she enjoyed shopping for fresh food and looked at these daily excursions as incorporating exercise into her life. I know she never left the kitchen messy and always completed a task once she started it. But how did she motivate herself to do all of this? She never appeared to be bitter about the work she did at home. She genuinely seemed to enjoy it.

But where would my experience as a young mother in California be different from Madame Chic's? Not everything that worked for her would work for me and vice versa. For example, the real Madame Chic would probably dismiss my talk about meditation and feng shui (although Madame Bohemienne probably wouldn't). Plus, even with my newly injected Parisian formalities, I am still a California girl at heart. How could I translate what I loved so much about my European experience to my American lifestyle?

You will learn much more about my sometimes bumpy journey to living well as a stay-at-home and work-at-home mom through the anecdotes in this book. I discovered that the stylish aspects of being chic only scratch the surface of what it means to thrive. I discovered that anyone, even overwhelmed stay-at-home mothers, could live well. Chic comes from within, continues at home, then goes with you throughout your day, touching those people you meet and blessing your life in the most amazing ways.

This book is divided into two sections: *Chez Vous* and *Les Routines de la Journée*. In *Chez Vous* we explore how to get your home in order and how to love it again. This first section presents a completely different approach to organizing and decluttering; it injects pleasure and peace into the process. It tackles mind blocks, attitudes, and underlying reasons why our homes are not in order.

The second part of the book, *Les Routines de la Journée*, is divided into three sections: the pleasures of the morning, the pleasures of the afternoon, and the pleasures of the evening. Here we get into the details that compose everyone's day—the details that no one talks about but that actually hold great meaning and significance. It covers everything from how we wake up in the morning to how we organize breakfast the night before. These details can turn your day from irritating to enjoyable.

There are a lot of tips in this book. You might use all of the tips, or you might only use some of them. I don't do everything mentioned here on a daily basis, but when I'm having a difficult moment in my day, I use the ideas in this book like a toolbox. Everyday life can be messy and, yes, it can be hard. But you are not alone, and you don't have to suffer through it. You can actually enjoy it. *All of it.* All of life's glorious messiness—the *is*ness of every single experience.

So are you ready to go on this journey? Let's get into it and enjoy every moment. As Mr. Satterthwaite would say, "Shall we?"

Part 1

CHEZ VOUS

Chapter 1

THE FRENCH CONNECTION

Famille Chic's traditional Sixteenth Arrondissement apartment in Paris was a tidy, clutter-free, and refreshingly formal home. I say "refreshingly" because up until then, I had been so used to casual living. They had grand floor-to-ceiling windows, botanical-print draperies, upholstered armchairs (no sofa), an antique record player, and a formal dining table where they enjoyed dinner every evening. During my stay with them, I soon came to realize that one of the reasons they were able to live so well was because everything ran smoothly at home. Their home life was meticulously organized right down to the very last domestic detail. Now that I am running my home with two children of my own, I appreciate more than ever how well organized the Chics were.

But is it just Famille Chic who runs an efficient home? Or

is it a French thing in general? I believe many French people take both pride and pleasure in making a home. For them, homemaking is just one of the many joys in life. A well-run home is a necessity. They are in on the secret that a passionately pleasant home life sets you up for a very happy life in the outside world.

My next-door neighbors in Santa Monica rented out their apartment for an entire year to a French family. The husband in the French family was a university professor who was teaching at a nearby college in his sabbatical year. I quickly befriended his wife, the lovely Emmanuelle. She perfectly embodied all I had come to know and love about the French women I observed in France. Chic Parisian bob? Check. Fabulous skin? Check. No-makeup look? Check. But I don't want to make her sound like a walking cliché. She was a marvelously talented woman—a mother of two teenage boys who had a banking career back in France. Yes, she had a high-profile career, but she took her role in looking after her home just as seriously and relished the art of homemaking.

Soon after they arrived, Emmanuelle invited me over to her place for lunch. But not only did she invite me for lunch, she invited me to cook with her. We made a delightful feast together—salad, leek tart, and pear custard. Her house was neat and presentable. We had many more lunches together during the year she was in Santa Monica. Once she even hosted a large luncheon for all of her new American girl-friends.

There was no clutter in her temporary home. And, yes, clutter would be quite easy to acquire during one year. The vacuum cleaner routinely hummed. Delicious smells regularly wafted from her air vents to mine. Emmanuelle enjoyed homemaking. Sure, she was taking the year off from her banking job, but I got the feeling she ran an equally tight ship back in Paris.

My other Parisian-cum-Californian friends are just as domestically inclined. We became friends with one young couple when she and I gave birth to our first daughters on the same day. Again, she and her husband love to entertain, and the wife is a fabulous cook—she makes homemade cakes and crepes for mere playdates (much to my husband's delight). Their house has not an ounce of clutter, and is, quite frankly, a minimalist masterpiece. And both husband and wife have very demanding careers.

The most important thing I've learned from my French

friends is that they regard domestic matters with a positive attitude. They derive pleasure from even the most mundane tasks. They don't look at housework as a degrading thing that's not worthy of their time, but rather as a necessity that helps life run smoothly and pleasantly—especially if they have meaningful careers and a life outside of the home. So chic.

The French value an orderly home life, even in times of upheaval. In the opening sequence of my favorite film, *Amélie*, an elderly gentleman returns home from his best friend's funeral still dressed for the funeral service; shedding a few tears and clearly distraught, he opens his address book and erases his deceased friend's contact information. I believe this sequence is a tongue-in-cheek comment on French people's domestic eccentricities. It was a touching moment, and yet, rather telling. That man's address book would be organized and up-to-date, even in a time of deep mourning.

Later in the film, Amélie is distraught when she has missed an opportunity to confess her love to Nino Quincampoix. She does not to wallow on her bed, wearing sweatpants while watching bad made-for-TV movies, but, rather, she turns to her kitchen to make her favorite plum cake—

her tears of sorrow artistically wiped away by her floured hands.

So on the regular days, and the extraordinary days, take inspiration from the French and look at homemaking as a pleasurable pursuit. This attitude can turn you from a clueless homemaker to a domestic goddess in no time.

Chapter 2

FALL IN LOVE WITH YOUR HOME AGAIN

In her book *Parisian Chic*, Inès de la Fressange says a "Parisian's apartment is her château." I love this saying. It implies that we do not need to own a château to feel like we live in one. We can live well no matter where we dwell.

You might already love your home and know the value of appreciating it, but most people, at some point in their lives, go through a period of feeling dissatisfied with where they live. This is perfectly normal. It is human nature to want to upgrade. You might want to move to a safer neighborhood or to a home with a big backyard so you can fulfill your dream of growing vegetables. We must hold on to these dreams, but in the meantime we must not wish away the life we currently have.

The key is to appreciate where you live *now* and learn how to thrive there. It may not be easy. I say this from experience. My husband and I have gone through the whole spectrum of emotions about where we live.

We live in a Mediterranean-style town home in Santa Monica, California. It has three levels, each with a beautiful view of a silk floss tree that is awash with enchanting pink blooms every fall. (For this view we are lucky. It is rare to have a view of anything but your neighboring building in Santa Monica apartments.) We lived there happily for four years before we had our children . . . and then things changed.

After we had our two daughters, we started to obsess over moving into a larger house. We told ourselves we had "outgrown" our apartment. Toys were everywhere. The double stroller had to be parked by the front door, crowding the entryway. There were so many stairs to lug groceries up and down. There was clutter everywhere. We wanted more space. We wanted a garden. We wanted out!

During one of our moan sessions (because that is what we were doing, moaning), I paused for a moment and realized I felt bitter and small. It is good to ask yourself if what you are doing feels contractive or expansive—in essence, to follow your gut. And all of the complaining I was doing about my own home felt very contractive.

When we were newlyweds and first came upon our future home, my husband and I were enchanted. The town home was lovely *and* in a desirable location in Santa Monica. When it was on the market, there were multiple offers on the property. We put in an offer, and we got it! We beat the other offers. We were ecstatic. It would be our first home as a married couple.

Every night for the next month, while the place was in escrow, we would walk past our soon-to-be new home and observe it from the street. On these walks we'd often spot the family we'd bought it from. We saw them having family dinners by the open windows, the branches of the grand silk floss tree reaching into the house. Whenever the family looked out to the street below we would quickly carry on walking so as not to appear creepy. (We later became friends with the family we bought the house from. They are lovely people.)

When we finally moved, it was a pivotal moment in my life. I was the lady of the house, in my own home . . . that I *owned.* Life could not get better. The first morning I woke up early and made coffee in the kitchen. I opened the kitchen window as I had seen our predecessors do and let the branches of the enchanting silk floss tree reach inside. Then the most curious thing happened. A squirrel, who my daughters and I later dubbed Mr. Squirrel, hopped up to the iron window box and sat on the sill. It was a magical moment. I wondered if he was going to come inside. I was so giddy, I felt like offering him a cup of tea! It was the perfect omen, a lovely welcome to the neighborhood.

We spent the next few years decorating our house, renovating the bathroom and the closets and updating bits and pieces in the kitchen. Everyone who came to visit told us our home had so much light—that it was a great space. We listened to music often. We opened the windows to let the Santa Monica sea air purify our living room. We frequently held dinner parties.

So how did our magical Shangri-la become a dumping

ground we had outgrown? How had our domestic paradise turned into a place we couldn't even stand? The only thing that had changed, other than having two children, was our attitude. It stank!

After this very important gut check I changed my perspective. I needed to find a way to love our home again. Our chief complaint was that apartment living was inconvenient when you had two kids and a dog. We wanted more space and a backyard for the kids to run around in. Okay, fair enough. But I decided to look at things differently. I pointed out to my husband that our town home was very spacious, as town homes go. If we were in New York, Paris, or his native London, our town home would be a hot property, coveted by millionaires. (That's being a bit dramatic, but I was trying to make the point to my husband.) When I lived in Paris with an aristocratic family in the Sixteenth Arrondissement, they seemed to make apartment living work for them, and they had five children! If they could do it and thrive, why couldn't we?

Once we shifted our attitude, we decided to see what we could change to fix the "problems" we thought our home had. The double stroller that was crowding the entryway was moved to the second stair landing in our hallway. This was out of the way yet still accessible if we needed to pull it out, and it freed up all of that blocked space in the entryway of our home.

We didn't have a garden, but I decided to take care of the neglected plants on my patio and get the girls involved. After a few fun trips to the garden center, we donned our gardening gloves and hats and pruned, watered, and fertilized. We even brought some ladybugs home from the garden center to spread through our container garden to act as a natural pesticide. (That's what I call getting into it!) Our patio plants started to thrive, as did the geraniums on our balcony and in the window box. The herbs in our kitchen window box provided beautiful fragrance when we opened the window and were handy to snip off and use while cooking. In short, we could enjoy growing flowers and herbs even though we didn't have an outdoor garden space to call our own. We might even get into growing container vegetables next year . . . who knows?

2BHK

My cousin Kristy recently visited India on a trip for her work, where she interviewed Indian women about their home lives.

So many of the women she interviewed lived with their large families in very small one-bedroom apartments. She said that they all aspired to having "2BHK," which means two bedrooms, hall, and kitchen. For many of those women, 2BHK would be a complete dream. This story really hit me. Not only did we have 2BHK, but we also had a living room, an office, a patio, balcony, and room for a washer/dryer. So what exactly was I complaining about again? Yes, it was time to check my bad attitude at the door and replace it with gratitude.

It is all about attitude. Yes, we still want a more spacious home with a garden, but in the meantime we are not going to wish our life away being miserable when we really should be grateful for having so much.

Visit Your Home

Wherever you live, whether it is in a home you own, a rented apartment, or a dorm room, if you feel you have fallen out of love with your space, it is time to start appreciating it again. Try to look at it from someone else's perspective. While you might not appreciate your current situation, there are plenty of people who are less fortunate than you who would. It's time to think about all of the things that make you grateful for where you live. It's time to change your mind-set.

Remember your first walk-through before you moved in? You were focusing on the great architecture, the light pouring through the windows, and the high ceilings. You were focusing on the positive, and you convinced yourself this was the perfect place for you. Bearing this in mind, let's try an exercise. Walk through your front door and look at your home as if seeing it again for the first time. Focus on all of its greatness. Doing this exercise will have a twofold effect. You'll see all of the great aspects of your home that made you initially fall in love with it, and you'll also keenly notice where you've been neglecting your space.

The more you can love your home, the more you'll want to take care of it. Then magical changes can occur. Instead of leaving that heap of laundry in the corner of your pretty bedroom for days on end, you'll feel inspired to sort it and put it away. Instead of letting clutter accumulate on your fireplace mantel, you'll feel motivated to find a place for all of your belongings and make a pleasing arrangement of objects that are special to you. You'll start to feel motivated to do all of this on a regular basis. If you love your home and take care of it, it will love you back, filling you with pride.

⟶ Getting Motivated ⟵

Perhaps this is all feeling a bit overwhelming. I completely get it. It's not like you have endless amounts of time to devote to sorting out your home life, and it feels like you have an enormous mountain to climb. The wonderful news is, people can change. To quote Great-Aunt Alicia from the musical *Gigi*, "If I can do it, you can!" And, no, I did not wake up one day and become a domestic goddess. In fact, I'm still working on it. The great thing is, I'm enjoying the process.

Let me ask you something. Can you easily have guests over without feeling anxiety? If an old friend just happened to pop over unexpectedly, would you be able to enjoy the visit, or would you be kicking yourself because laundry is strewn all over the living room floor? Would you be completely comfortable with having overnight guests at the drop of a hat? What about friends staying in your home while you're not there? Would that spark feelings of panic?

The Chics would be able to have people over spontaneously without a problem because their home was run with the efficiency of a small hotel. There were no messes to conceal, no emergency cleaning sessions to undertake. Because their space was so clutter free, it was easy to clean. Never one to procrastinate, Madame Chic dealt with home maintenance issues as soon as they arose, and because of this, she didn't experience setbacks to her weekly routine. Remember, the Chics threw a dinner party at least once a week. They wouldn't be able to do this without stress if their home wasn't consistently tidy.

While my husband and I were on our yearly trip to England to visit his family, we met up with one of his old friends from school who said he was going to be visiting California a few days later with a friend. My husband, being very generous and completely clueless about my anxiety about having people over when everything isn't perfect (okay, not even close to being perfect), invited his friends to stay at our house while we were in England. My insides immediately seized up.

What state had I left the house in? We'd left in a bit of a hurried mess. They would be using the guest bedroom. When was the last time I had changed those sheets? They'd need to put new ones on. What was the state of the linen cupboard? Was there clutter everywhere? How clean were the bathrooms? Oh dear, his friends were going to learn about our horrendous housekeeping skills.

His friends had a lovely time. I'm sure they didn't care too much about the state of our home and were just grateful to have a place to stay. But the stress I felt about their visit—this was clearly before I started learning to cultivate inner peace—provided the motivation I needed to start sorting out my home when I got back.

So if you need that extra push, you can use a similar motivation, but with a twist. Invite overnight houseguests to stay with you. Or schedule a party to be thrown in your home. Is your house in the state you'd like it to be in? What changes would you make?

Here's the twist: make the changes because you are excited about your impending houseguests and want to make their stay comfortable, not because you're afraid of what they'll think of you. Then when you're mopping the floor in the guest bathroom, you'll be doing it to make your guests' stay as lovely as possible, not because you're worried they'll judge you if there is dust on the baseboard. So schedule the date for your overnight guests. This deadline will motivate you to get on your feet and get stuff done. Just remember: no matter what you accomplish, it's all good. Your guests will love you no matter what, so enjoy the process.

Chic Motivational Tips

- *Play music while you clean and organize. Music injects energy into the whole process.*

- *Listen to an audiobook. Audiobooks run for hours. Think about how much you can accomplish while listening to a riveting story.*

- *Time yourself while you clean. Figure out how much time you want to devote to caring for your home, set the timer, and get going. Don't forget the music!*

- *Assess and celebrate your progress. When you see visual evidence that your home is getting in order, you will feel the push to persevere. Don't stop now!*

⌁ No More Neglect ⌁

Take your first step by getting your home ready for a single event, such as a dinner party. Do what it takes to make your home ready for your guests: clear the clutter, dust those surfaces, spruce up the powder room. Do what you need to do. This single event will show you what needs to be done on a regular basis to keep your home ready for any future spontaneous guests. Take note of what you needed to accomplish to get ready for the dinner party and then make sure that you add these items to your weekly to-do list. After incorporating these tasks into your cleaning routine on a regular basis, you will have established the routines you need to graduate to the next level. Your home will then be ready for a last-minute cup of tea with your neighbor or comfortable weekend stay for your great-aunt Sally.

POWDER ROOM CHECKLIST

It's always a good idea to have your powder room ready for guests. This room is really easy to keep up because its function is so simple. There should not be any clutter to deal with. Just make sure the toilet and sink are always spotlessly clean and that the hand towels are regularly refreshed. Add luxurious hand soap, a fancy room spray of some sort, and a little vase of flowers. Keep plenty of tissue and toilet paper on hand. Have fun decorating this room too. Go for it: wallpaper, unusual sconces, artwork. It's a tiny little room that shows your home's character. Your guests will be charmed when they use it.

Help!

Let's start by assessing your help situation. Do you have a housekeeper? A helpful family or roommate? Do you live by yourself and have no help at all? Well, the good news is, if you live by yourself, you don't have to pick up after anyone, so it will be quite easy to implement your new routines. If you live with a family and they are not helpful now, they need to become helpful. If your children are old enough to have chores—and I feel you can never start too young—by all means delegate. This goes for your spouse too. You should not be expected to do everything with regard to keeping up your home. Sit everyone down for a family meeting. Provide cake and tea—this helps to ease tensions—and decide what each family member will be responsible for.

If you have a housekeeper, make sure you go over in detail what you need help with. Even if your housekeeper only comes once every two weeks, it is good to let him or her know the job expectations. In her book *Domestic Bliss,* Rita Konig writes, "It would be unthinkable to employ new staff in your office and show them to their desks on the first day, show them where the kettle and the bathroom are and then never give them any more direction, so the same rules should apply at home." So if you have any kind of domestic staff, show them how you like things done. Give them adequate training for their jobs. You are paying them, after all. Don't be shy!

 Systems

Take a look at your typical weekly schedule and assign your chores to the days that make the most sense. Tailor this routine to your life. Don't tailor your life to the routine. Don't schedule so many tasks that you have no freedom or time to enjoy your family. Pretend you are the manager of a hotel and are assigning duties to your staff. Once you make a schedule that works for you, rarely deviate from the plan.

Sample cleaning schedule

Monday: Laundry (darks and delicates), dust, vacuum, mop floors, empty all trash

Tuesday: Laundry (whites and towels), ironing, bathrooms

Wednesday: Dust, vacuum, wash windows, change children's sheets

Thursday: Kitchen detail cleaning, empty all trash

Friday: Change master bedroom sheets, dust, vacuum

This is only a sample weekly schedule. As you can see, a little is done every day except for weekends. Your schedule will probably be different. Maybe you'd like to devote two entire days to cleaning, for example. Again, please note that not everything on this schedule should have to be completed by you. Delegate. Children can empty trash and dust their rooms. Hire the teenager next door to do your ironing. I have our cleaning schedule posted on the inside of the cabinet where we keep our cleaning supplies. This way, no matter who is doing the housework, they know what needs to get done on any given day.

Needless to say, there are things that need to be done every day: the dishes, a general tidy-up of the kitchen and living room, making the beds, and keeping the bathroom straight. But it will all be so much easier and take less time if you can stick to a regular cleaning schedule.

Cleaning schedule for working people

If you are working outside of the home, you will still need to accomplish all the tasks on the previous cleaning schedule, but you'll have to get creative about when they are accomplished. Try to incorporate some chores in your busy weekday to avoid devoting all Saturday afternoon to the housekeeping. You work hard during the week and deserve to rest over the weekend. If you stick to the schedule and rarely stray from it, these tasks will become habits you accomplish effortlessly.

It should again be noted that the kitchen should be clean at the end of every day. It is a good idea to add a detailed kitchen cleaning to your list once a week that includes cleaning the inside of the refrigerator and microwave and mopping the floors.

Sunday: Empty all trash, do any necessary ironing for the week ahead.

Monday: Laundry. After you wake up, put a load of delicates in the washing machine. When finished, hang dry delicates. Then pop another load of clothes into the washer. When you return from work, put wet clothes into dryer. If needed, put another load of clothes into washer. Fold when dry. Sweep kitchen floor and entryway.

Tuesday: Repeat before-work washing/after-work drying and folding with your whites. In the morning before your shower, wipe down surfaces of your bathroom. Clean tub and toilet, mop floor.

Wednesday: Vacuum living room carpet before going to work (you'll come home to a beautiful carpet!). Pop the children's sheets into the washer. Put fresh sheets on their beds (unless, of course, they are old enough to do this themselves). Take a slightly damp cloth and dust the surfaces of your living room.

Thursday: Launder towels and bath mats before work and dry when you get home. Dust and clean guest bathroom/powder room in the evening. Detailed kitchen cleaning.

Friday: Launder master bedroom sheets before work. Place in dryer when you get home. Always have two sets of bedding so you can make your bed with fresh sheets while the others are being laundered (but do try to let your mattress air out for at least twenty minutes before replacing sheets). This way you come home to a well-made bed after a long day at the office. In the morning, clear and dust bedroom surfaces.

Every other Saturday: Wash windows.

A major key to the schedule for working people is delegation. For example, your husband can be in charge of bathrooms and vacuuming, while you are responsible for laundry and the daily kitchen clean. Your kids can do the dusting and empty the trash.

CHIC HOUSEPLANTS

Orchids

If you know how to care for them, orchids are ideal houseplants. Their exotic blooms that last for months on end add exquisite beauty to your home. Place your orchid in a light-filled room away from direct sunlight. Water them once a week, allowing the water to drain through the pot. Never let orchids sit in stagnant water or their roots will rot. It is for this reason that I usually keep the orchid in the plastic pot it came in and simply place that in a decorative pot. Once a week I take my orchids out of the decorative pot and proceed with watering, adding orchid food to the water once every two weeks for healthier blooms. Once the water has drained, I place the orchid in its container back in the pretty pot. For an even easier watering method, just place two ice cubes on the moss or bark at the base of your orchid once a week. Once the orchid blooms have fallen off, don't give up on it! Continue to water and care for your orchid, trimming back any dead leaves and stems, and your precious plant might bloom again in a few months.

African Violets

African violets are some of the easiest houseplants to keep if you follow their simple requirements. My grandparents loved African violets and kept them all over their house, so they evoke strong memories from my childhood. Their cheerful little blooms will blossom year-round and make a charming addition to any home. I find that purchasing pots specifically made for African violets is the best way to make them last. Never get water on the leaves of an African violet, which may cause brown spots to form. Instead, water African violets from beneath by adding water three-quarters of the way up in the base of the violet pot. Then put African-violet potting mix in the porous top half of the pot. Place the top half of the pot in the water, and position your plant out of direct sunlight. Check the water levels every two weeks and replace with fresh water. Place a few drops of African violet plant food in the water for even more abundant blooms.

Ferns

For rooms in your home that don't have a lot of natural light, ferns make ideal houseplants. They were all the rage for the Victorians, who thought they cured madness and boosted one's love life. Ferns also evoke the timeless quality of a bygone era (think dinosaurs). Ferns love humidity, so mist them regularly with water. Always keep the soil damp but not soaked so that the roots don't rot, and be sure to feed them with a weak fertilizer once a month.

⌁ The Details ⌁

Once your housekeeping schedule is working, you can start to have fun with the details. Your home is an art exhibit and you are the curator. It reflects your personality and your style. When you get dressed in the morning, you choose little things like earrings and shoes to complete the outfit. In your home, you get to decide everything, from how you'd like your towels folded to how you like to make your bed. Some people might say, "I don't have the time to think about such insignificant things," but I actually believe if you decide how you want tasks to be done and stick with it, you can save yourself time in the long run and create an aesthetically pleasing environment to live in.

This is where simple pleasures are born. It's the small things that can bring so much joy into your day. You will never feel bored or restless when doing housework if you take pleasure and pride in the details of how it's done.

These details are also the key to making you the connoisseur of your own home. You will know your home so intimately and derive so much pleasure from it that you will become the expert on your home life. Your family will remember you for these details. Long after your children are grown and out of the house, they will appreciate those details that you took such care with, and when they are running their own homes, they will remember that and want to create lasting impressions of their own for their families.

HOW TO FOLD A TOWEL

Here's an example that gives me so much pleasure. I learned how to fold towels from British television presenter Anthea Turner. Please, no scoffing. Or as my husband would say, no contempt prior to investigation. Once you fold your towels this way, you will never go back.

Start with your towel lying flat. Fold the towel in thirds lengthwise. Then take the long ends and fold them to meet in the middle. Finally, flip the towel over one more time and lay that delightfully plump towel in your cupboard with the two folds facing the rear. Now when you open your cupboard, you will see a sumptuous stack of towels worthy of the Ritz. This takes no more time than it would to sloppily fold and stick the towel in the cupboard, and it actually makes it easier to grab towels on the go and not mess up the entire stack. There is a method to this madness.

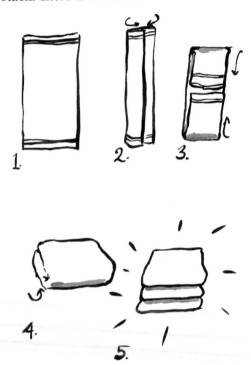

⟳ This Is Not a Race ⟳

In the beginning, devote one hour a day to getting your home in order and your system running. It will take as long as it takes. This is not a race and you are not behind. Just tackle everything with *joie de vivre*. Don't think of this process as a chore but as a wonderful expression of how much you appreciate everything you have. Remember what Ralph Waldo Emerson said: "Life is a journey, not a destination." Don't tell yourself you will only be happy once you get your home in order. You might never feel that your home is perfectly in order. With the ebb and flow of everyday life, your home will constantly need love and attention. Just commit to enjoying the process now. *Everything*.

When you've pulled hundreds of clothes out of your closet and are staring at intimidating piles that you need to sort through, enjoy it. When you and your husband are sweating from moving the furniture around to try to give your living room a new lease on life, enjoy that too. When you are finally going through that pile of dishes in the sink that has been sitting there for a day, enjoy it. Because what is the alternative? Misery? Why waste time being miserable? This journey we are embarking on is exciting. It is the pathway to a new life that began when you started reading this book.

This is not a race. The destination is not important. It is in the journey where all of the critical steps are taken. So enjoy this, my friend. Because life is meant to be celebrated. *All of it.*

Chapter 3

CLUTTER

⌒◦ Clutter (Mental and Physical) ◦⌒

The clutter has got to go. I think we can all agree upon that. But then we procrastinate. We say we will get to this later. It's only temporary. But then temporary turns from days to weeks to months and soon this clutter has become a fixture—a design element, if you will, and an unwelcome one at that.

Before we know it, we have little piles everywhere. Piles of semisorted mail; piles of clothes that need to be donated to charity; piles of scrapbook supplies; piles of old magazines that you plan on going through to cut out pictures for your vision board (don't try to deny it); piles of miscellaneous things that, like magnets, become attracted to each other. Piles!

Every time you look at these piles, you are reminded of work you have to do. You even beat yourself up a little. You make a promise to yourself that you will do it. But when you get a spare moment, you are so exhausted that you would rather do *anything* than sort through those piles. So instead you make a cup of tea and watch a show on TV and put it out of your mind. But the piles are still there. Oh well. One day.

Listen, I don't want you to feel overwhelmed, because I know exactly how that feels. I had been doing pretty well with clutter clearing. I was really keeping a manageable hold on the clutter. Well, most of the clutter. I would say about 80 percent of the clutter in my home I was able to keep at bay. I developed clutter-busting systems and stuck to them. I kept my hot spots and stagnant spaces clear, which we'll discuss in a moment. But for some reason, there were certain areas of my home where I just couldn't kick the clutter. I knew the root of my problem was deep, and if I had this problem, a lot of other people must have it too.

So I did what any other angst-ridden housewife in Santa Monica would do: I consulted a feng shui expert! My friend Nicole is just such a person, and we had a long talk. She told me that so many clutter issues stem from a scarcity mind-set—the unconscious belief that we need to hold on to things in case something bad happens. We tell ourselves we need our possessions, and we cling to them mentally and physically.

Nicole was right. It's funny because, deep down, I already knew this. I am worried that if I throw something away, I will need it again. I also have what is commonly referred to as bag-lady syndrome. Even though things are good now, I am waiting for the other shoe to drop. Hey, if times get tough, I might need all my stuff!

I always say that awareness is the first step. Now that I am aware of my scarcity mind-set, I know why I resist getting rid of something. The truth is, we need very little, yet we have so much. Opening my eyes to these unconscious negative beliefs has highlighted the clutter around my house. I look at those little piles as a challenge. I stare those piles in the face. I can and will conquer those piles, and you can too.

Take a manageable amount of time—whatever you can commit to on a daily basis—and begin to tackle clutter with relish. If you can commit to fifteen minutes a day, wonderful! If you can commit to an hour, fabulous! If you don't want to commit to a definite time, just tell yourself you will tackle one pile a day. The more you get in the practice of clearing your clutter, the more you develop an eye for spotting it.

Hot Spots

My number one clutter-busting rule is this: above all else, always keep your hot spot(s) clear. Hot spots are the areas in your home that tend to always develop clutter. They are most likely in high-traffic areas of your home. Our hot spots are the dining room table, the stairs, the entryway table, and the bench at the foot of our bed. They will be different for everyone.

You know what it's like. You've been out all day with the kids. You bring in your handbag, the mail, your sunglasses,

and your ereader. You set these things down on the first surface you see: the entryway table. You get distracted because
the kids need help washing their hands and the dog needs
to be let out. Oh, and you weren't the only one who brought
things into the house. The kids placed their artwork from
school and a few miscellaneous rocks they picked up from
your walk on the table too. Your husband played golf that
afternoon and left a handful of wooden golf tees, his receipts,
extra change, and golf hat all on this now glorious pile on
your entryway table. What once was a clear space now holds
everything from your handbag to golf paraphernalia to glitter
paper and rocks. Sigh.

Much of this can be solved by simply having a place to
put your things when you get home. A shelf in the hall closet
for your handbag. A hook for your keys. A rack for the hats.
A desk for the artwork. It will take a few more seconds to put
everything in its proper space, but once you do, this hot spot
will be cleared.

Other hot spots also tend to soak up transient clutter—
clutter that just happens to pass by throughout our busy days.
For example, our dining room is also our living room. And,
oh yes, this space is also the playroom. So we find the most

random assortment of belongings on our dining room table at any given moment. Books, hair bows, sunscreen, children's toothbrushes (I know), receipts, paperwork, dog biscuits, and empty cups of tea are the kinds of things you might find there.

I used to resign myself to it. I would tell myself (save for the empty cups of tea and the odd paper here and there) that none of that mess was mine. I would blame it on other people. I had become used to it. When I started loving my home again, that hot-spot clutter stood out to me like a peeling nail in an otherwise perfect manicure. If Madame Chic saw my dining room table, she would probably stare at it in utter confusion. In her home, every piece of furniture had a specific function and the dining room table was for food, flowers, candles, and tableware. Anything not related to fine dining wouldn't be caught dead on her table.

Now, several times a day, I clear off the dining room table. If I am passing by it and see something that does not belong, I pick it up and put it away on the way to wherever I'm going. Yes, it requires constant editing, but hot spots do.

Then I noticed something very peculiar. The more I cleared our dining room table hot spot, the less stuff accumulated on it. My husband started putting his things in "his" bowl. (I keep a blue-willow-patterned antique bowl for him to put his change, wallet, golf balls, etc. in. I cover it with a vintage linen pillowcase to hide the unsightliness of it all.) My husband is now on board. My girls will now grow up with a clear dining room table, and they are less likely to clutter theirs when they are older. The ripple effects of keeping your hot spots clear are marvelous and vast.

Let's try an exercise. Go to your hot spot. Right now. I'm serious. Go have a look. What is on it? I bet it is a miscellaneous assortment of random items. When you have small children, sometimes these items will inspire in you a combination of exasperation and the giggles. Let's get real. It's time to clear that hot spot, now and tomorrow and the next day. Yes, you have to keep going back, but the clutter will be less and less over time. I promise.

Constantly clearing the clutter in your hot spots will become second nature to you, no longer a chore, but just a way of life. You're passing by the playroom on the way to the living room (or in my case, just walking a few feet), so you might as well pick up the magnetic fishing boat toy and put it in its rightful place. This is not to say that your children won't learn to pick up after themselves. They will. It's just that you are leading by example.

～⊙ Stagnant Spaces ⊙～

Stagnant spaces are the out-of-the-way areas in your home that attract clutter. If you've read *Lessons from Madame Chic*, you know how much I love to edit my wardrobe and donate old clothes. Each season I go through all my clothes and decide what to donate to charity. I usually keep a black garbage bag under my vanity that holds all of the clothes I plan on dropping off at the Goodwill. I fill the bag and then tell my husband to put any clothes he wants to donate in the bag. He is not as motivated as I am in this department, and every third day or so I'll see an item of his clothing on top of the bag. Then I tell myself that I better go through the baby's clothes. Soon this unsightly and rather stuffed black garbage bag has been sitting under the vanity in my bedroom for well over a month.

Stagnant spaces are out of the way, and because of this we are less likely to think about them. But the clutter in our stagnant spaces affects us as much as the clutter in the hot spots does. The sight of it infiltrates our psyche, and because we might not be actively thinking about it every day, we definitely become used to it.

Now have a look at your stagnant spaces. They can be in the

most curious places. If you have small children, they could be out-of-reach places like the mantelpiece or the top of a bookshelf. You store things there "temporarily," but then you forget about them. Soon you have thermometers, bottles of soap, playing cards, and an iPad on your fireplace mantel. *Pas chic!*

Stagnant spaces can also lurk inside your drawers. We all have one or two junk drawers, but it is nice to organize these a little. You can make dividers out of old stationery boxes, business card boxes, anything like that. You don't have to spend a fortune at the Container Store. See how you can organize your drawers with what you already have in your house. Aim to organize one drawer a day, or one a month. Are all of the drawers in my house perfect? No. But they aren't in unorganized shambles either. Even the junk drawers have a certain rhyme and reason to them.

Stay on top of your stagnant spaces and, like your hot spots, over time you will notice that you have hardly any clutter at all.

Part 2

LES ROUTINES DE LA JOURNÉE

Chapter 4

THE PLEASURES
OF THE MORNING

The other day I was standing in a long line at my local coffee-house in Santa Monica, Caffe Luxxe. (This is also where I often to go write.) There were four women in front of me, all interestingly turned out, I might add—people watching provides me endless pleasure during the day as well—and the woman who was at the front of the line was ordering a pastry. The man working behind the counter asked her a question to clarify her order. He had asked her something like "Would you like the one with cheese?" She misheard him and thought he had asked her, "What are your basic needs?"

She seemed a bit taken aback and repeated, "What are my basic needs?" There was a moment of silence as she contemplated this and then, after a beat, all six of us (including the barista), started to laugh. A deep guttural laugh. The idea of being asked such an intimate question before the hour of nine a.m. in a public place by a complete stranger was so absurd. The woman next to me said, "Well, for me it's food, water, and shelter." We continued to laugh. I laughed until I cried. In that moment I was so happy to be laughing with these strangers, all coming together and partaking in a little levity before our day began. It is a wonderful thing to be present and connect with the people around you, even if you've never met them before. It is moments like these that make life wonderful. And all before my first cup of coffee. Every morning holds the promise that today will be remarkable. Yes, even for you non-morning people. Even if you feel you've done the same thing every day for the past thirty years, you never know what could happen today. What are you looking forward to?

I look forward to pulling back the curtains after I wake up to see what the day looks like. I am one of those kooky people who talk to their plants, so I also chime out a "Bonjour!" to my container rosebushes, jasmine, and geraniums, and water them if needed. I always open the windows to air out each bedroom that has been slept in. I do the same in the living room and kitchen to allow in the cool morning sea air.

For many people, the pleasures of morning include smelling their freshly brewed coffee or tea and having that first sip. Seeing your family and saying good morning to them, especially to your kids, can warm your heart. My husband gets up a little later than I do, and while I probably annoy him deeply every morning, I look forward to giving him a kiss and a cuddle and saying, "Good morning, bud," in my chipper voice before he's quite woken up. He's one of those self-professed non-morning people.

My mother likes to watch her morning news show as she gets ready for the day. That is a big pleasure for her. My father likes to get up early—five a.m.!—and read the *Los Angeles Times*. He's done this for as long as I can remember. We all have different routines in the morning that help us get ready for the day.

But I am getting ahead of myself . . . first you have to wake up.

⟳ Waking Up ⟲

How you wake up every morning can affect the rest of your day. We've all heard the saying "She woke up on the wrong side of the bed," and we know how that feels. When I was in high school, I had to wake up at five every morning for "zero period" band practice. I had an alarm clock that produced the most dreadful noise, *EEE EEE EEE*. I can't believe I even used that thing for more than a day. A few years later, when I finally had more sense, I found a more soothing alarm clock that woke me up with the sound of Tibetan bells. This was much nicer, and the bells progressed from soft to loud over a manageable period of time.

All that changed after I had my two girls. When I heard them stirring around six a.m., I would groan and check my iPhone for the time. Then I would quickly check my email and maybe even read a few headline newsclips from CNN. All in the space of five minutes—right after I'd woken from a deep sleep. My still-sleepy brain would be inundated with work demands, murders, wars, and advertisements. Whoa. Long gone were the days when I woke up to Tibetan bells and seemingly floated out of bed as they gradually rang louder. The fact that I have kids makes it imperative that I get up on the right side of the bed. But waking up and then immediately checking my email did not give my body the time to slowly reboot.

Yes, we must take it slow when we wake up. Pause to calm yourself down and prepare for the day ahead. Lie in bed and take a few deep breaths. It would be a fantastic idea to do some stretches. Even trying to touch your toes for thirty seconds counts. I sit on the floor with my feet stretched out in front of me, touch my toes, and bow my head down while taking deep breaths. I really feel the stretch in the back of my neck. I also like to sit with one leg crossed on the floor in front of the other and then bend over as far as I can to touch the floor with both hands and forehead, breathing deeply. Then I cross my legs the other direction and repeat. These deep breathing stretches are a palate cleanser, if you will, and help to smooth the transition from sleep to wakefulness.

After stretching, you could step outside and take a deep breath of fresh air. Or simply open a window. You could say an affirmation and repeat it three times. You can put on your fluffy robe and warm slippers and appreciate their caressing texture. Whatever you do, do something to remind yourself that you are alive.

∽⊙ Affirmations ⊙∾

Affirmations are positive phrases you say to yourself. I have found that affirmations have improved the quality of my life. They are verbal vision boards that help make your dreams come true. I find the best times to say affirmations are right before an important event, when you're in the midst of a difficult situation, and right before you get out of bed.

To say affirmations out loud, you need to put all self-consciousness aside. But you don't *have* to speak them out loud. You can just think them and feel them. So you don't need to worry about your spouse thinking you've gone crazy when you repeat joyously, three times in a row, "I am healthy, prosperous, and efficient!"

I don't say affirmations every day, but I do say them pretty often. If I feel completely exhausted and have a sense of impending doom about the unavoidable nonstop twelve hours of watching the kids, cleaning the house, and work I have ahead of me, I will definitely say something like "I am vibrant, full of energy, and ready to take on this day."

Maybe you wake up and the voice in your head immediately tells you that you're exhausted and you can't face the day. Or you wake up and instantly think of a problem brewing at work and feel dread, letting the issue already ruin your day. Or you wake up and remember that you're still ten pounds overweight and tell yourself some unloving thing like "I'm not pretty enough."

We've all been there.

If we can believe these negative thoughts so strongly, why can't we believe the positive ones? Who says you don't have the energy for the day? Who says you aren't beautiful enough? Who says this problem at work is going to ruin your week? It's all about attitude, and if you affirm something positive and not only believe it but *feel* it in your bones, you are shining light into the darkness.

Powerful Affirmations

. . . .

I am vibrant, healthy, and full of energy.

My beauty is radiant.

I am a calm and patient parent.

Today I will relish the small things.

Today I will make my home beautiful.

I choose to eat healthful foods today.

My home is a sanctuary.

I can remain effortlessly in the present moment.

My creativity is inspiring.

I can get through any situation with grace.

No matter what happens today, I will cultivate inner peace.

I can change the world.

All is well.

These are just a few. But how uplifting is it to tell yourself at six a.m. that you can change the world and truly believe it?

If you are not accustomed to saying affirmations, you will feel ridiculous at first, but stick with it. You can change the negative tape that loops in your head every day, I promise. This is a secret to becoming chic. You know that mysterious *je ne sais quoi* we were talking about before? An affirmative attitude is a part of it. Chic people seem to have it together. They have an almost otherworldliness about them. It's because they don't buy into the negative hype and aren't always racked with neurosis. It's their delicious secret.

CANDLES FOR THE MORNING

Use fresh, invigorating scents in the morning to awaken your sense of smell and get you excited about the day. I love to use floral or fruity garden scents in the morning such as:

rose

tuberose

grapefruit

gardenia

lime

violet

lemon verbena

⌁ Wake-up Time ⌁

If you feel like you wake up every morning and are immediately playing catch-up, perhaps you should wake up a little earlier to accomplish everything you need to. If this feels unbearable, consider going to bed earlier. It's a simple math equation. Figure out the time you need to wake up to accomplish all that needs to be done in the morning, subtract how many hours of sleep you need to feel rested (normally eight), and you end up at what time you should be going to bed.

We all have different things that need to get done in the morning. The most important thing is to pause right after you wake up. You'll learn throughout this book how important I think gratitude is. And no matter the circumstance, I never get out of bed without first saying a prayer of thanks. In fact, "thank you" is the last thing I say before going to sleep and the first thing I say before getting up. I don't put my feet on the ground without thinking *and* feeling it. Giving thanks can truly fill your heart with love. Even on the darkest days, there are always things to be thankful for.

Now that I have children and most of those newborn sleepless nights are behind us (*merci*), I wake up around forty-five minutes before the rest of the family. During this time I get up in a slow and luxurious manner. I lie in bed for a few moments and think about the day ahead. Then I do a fifteen-minute meditation. If I need to pump myself up for something, I say my affirmations to myself. I stretch a little by doing a twist or two. I open the patio doors and water my plants. I drink a tall glass of water.

I also start to get ready for the day during this period. Because it is very important to me to look presentable, I use this time for my toilette. I can take a shower or bath, apply a no-makeup look (more on this later), and pick out my clothes.

Some days this doesn't happen. Some days the girls wake up early and I have to go to the kitchen in my pajamas to get breakfast started. I go with the flow.

A Place for Our Morning Things

What do you use in the morning? Coffee? Sugar? Toaster? Dog leash? Do you store these things in places that make sense and help your morning run more smoothly? First we must find the most logical place to keep the things we need in the morning, and then we must get in the habit of putting these things away in their proper places.

You will know your morning things are not well organized if you feel frustration during any part of your morning routine. For example, if you have to travel to four locations just to make a cup of coffee (coffee machine, silverware drawer, refrigerator, and cupboard for sugar), place everything in the same vicinity to make getting that vital cup of coffee as easy as possible. Keep the bread bin by the toaster. Keep the dog leash on a hook by your coat. Make it as easy as possible to clean up after yourself. Otherwise, the dog leash might get carelessly thrown in the shoe basket and the milk might spoil because it was forgotten and left out of the refrigerator.

Make it a habit to put things away as soon as you're finished with them. Try not to leave them all out for one epic cleaning at the end of the day; this is how we come to feel overwhelmed. And, yes, I speak from experience.

ALBUMS FOR THE MORNING

Les invités by Accordéon Mélancolique, Sterkenburg Records, 2008.

Start the day off in Paris (even if only in your mind) by listening to this classic French music.

Kreisler Plays Kreisler, Charles O'Connell, Donald Voorhees, Victor Symphony Orchestra & Carl Lamson, BMG, 1997.

Make breakfast to this classical violin album and prepare to be charmed.

Bach for Breakfast: The Leisurely Way to Start Your Day (compilation) Philips, 1995.

Spend breakfast with Bach and let these leisurely melodies set the tone for the day.

Cabo Verde by Cesária Évora, Lusafrica, 1997.
This upbeat album will make you want to samba through the rest of your day.

Pierre Lapointe, Audiogram, 2004.
Feel optimistic and get inspired with this delightfully romantic French album.

The Guitar Collection—Flamenco by Salsa Rosso, Red Sauce Records, 2005.
Get things moving with this flamenco collection that will prompt you to add passion to your morning routine.

 Getting Dressed

In *Lessons from Madame Chic* we were introduced to the ten-item wardrobe—that fabulous capsule collection of high-quality clothing where all pieces live in harmony. Now that you have cleared out the clutter in your closet and whittled down to the ten-item wardrobe (or a size that is workable for you), getting dressed will be such a breeze. Check the weather report, even if you think you know what the weather will be like. Now it's time to pick out your clothes for the day. This is so simple because your core items are all interchangeable.

SAMPLE TEN-ITEM WARDROBES

Spring

2 lightweight sweaters
1 pair white jeans
1 pair tan slacks
3 lightweight knit dresses
3 blouses

Spring Extras: **T-shirts**, lightweight cardigans, trench coat, lightweight jacket, blazers, lightweight scarves, sandals, ballet flats, heels, jewelry, sunglasses, hair accessories.

Summer

. . . .

3 blouses

1 pair white jeans

1 pair light denim jeans

4 summer dresses

1 skirt or pair of shorts

Summer Extras: T-shirts, layering tank tops, lightweight sweaters, lightweight cardigans, blazers, voluminous scarves, beachwear, sandals, espadrilles, leather flip-flops, heels, jewelry, sunglasses.

Fall/Winter

. . . .

I have combined fall and winter here because the type of clothing used will be similar for both seasons. Feel free to switch out the blouses and dresses to add variety as you head into winter. If you live in a very cold climate and cannot wear dresses in the winter, change them out for more jeans and sweaters. Adapt this model to your personal circumstances.

3 blouses

3 (+) sweaters

> *1 pair dark denim jeans*
> *1 pair black skinny jeans or black slacks*
> *2 dresses*
>
> *Fall/Winter Extras: T-shirts, extra sweaters if needed, extra pair of jeans if needed, cardigans, scarves, gloves, jackets, heavy coat, tights, boots, ballet flats, heels, jewelry, sunglasses.*

But hold on a second—what is that distracting chatter at the back of your mind? This is always the moment in the day when our subconscious tries to talk us out of wearing our best. You run all of the things you have to do for the day through your mind. You realize that the only time you will be going outside will be to drop off and pick up the kids from school and perhaps to run to the supermarket. You might try to convince yourself to wear exercise clothes because that is what you are used to. You are not making a stylish impression when wearing exercise clothes. You just blend into the crowd.

I once overheard two mothers talking outside of my older daughter's school. One said to the other, who was wearing a tennis outfit, "Are you playing tennis after this?" The other mother responded, "Oh no. I haven't played in years. This is just what I'm wearing today."

Now is the time to break those old habits. Sure, you might be accustomed to wearing exercise clothes all day long (even if you haven't actually exercised at all). But now you have a well-thought-out capsule wardrobe. It's just as easy to pull out the silk blouse and dark-wash jeans as it is to grab the Lycra leggings and tank top. If you feel anxious about wearing a nice blouse while cooking or cleaning, simply pop an apron on top of your clothes while at home. That was one of Madame Chic's secrets for remaining stylish and keeping her clothes stain free throughout the day.

If you find yourself in a major rush in the mornings, it's a good idea to select your clothes the night before. When you are compiling your ten-item wardrobe, take pictures of outfit combinations and keep them on your phone. Or print digital photos and tape them on the inside of your closet doors. But truly, once the clutter is cut and you have curated a select few items, the cloud of confusion around getting dressed will dissipate. Over time you will become accustomed to wearing nice clothes every day, even if you have nowhere special to go.

My next-door neighbors in Santa Monica have rented

out their town home for a year again, this time to a Norwegian family. The mother of the family is another Madame Chic. She is a simply stunning woman of a certain age and dresses well every day. She even wears a dress while she rides her bike! She makes it work. She and I enjoy speaking every time we meet. We got into a conversation about clothes, and she said she noticed that Californians are very casual in their daily wardrobe and she found it interesting that I was not. She said she noticed that Californians are also very laid-back and friendly, and perhaps their clothing reflected that. This got me thinking. Yes, we Americans do pride ourselves on being open and friendly. We don't think of ourselves as stuffy and unapproachable. Wouldn't we want our clothes to be as appealing as our friendliness? Wouldn't it be possible to dress a little more formally while still maintaining our famously open attitude?

Embrace Your Femininity

If you equate being home doing chores and looking after the children with drudgery, then you will probably dress accordingly—wandering around the house in sweatpants or perhaps not even getting out of your pajamas. You might pull your hair back in a careless ponytail. What is the point of looking good if you are going to be scrubbing toilets and wiping runny noses? When you have a baby and are feeling exhausted and overwhelmed, it's easy to get into the habit of not caring how you present yourself. Soon years have passed and you've been wandering around in a constant state of frumpiness. You can't imagine wearing a pretty summer dress when you aren't going to work or don't have any special plans. You might feel self-conscious, as though people are judging you for dressing up during the day.

Perhaps when you dress up, you feel as though you are drawing attention to yourself. You don't want compliments; you just want to fly under the radar. If you wander around in jeans and a T-shirt every single day, then you won't cause a stir. No one will notice you haven't quite lost the baby weight yet. No one will look closely at the dark circles under your eyes.

Does any of this resonate with you? If so, it's time to set aside all of those inhibitions and embrace your femininity. Start with small steps. Challenge yourself to wear your pretty summer dress even if you don't have special plans (especially if you don't have special plans). Do something different with your hair. Brush it and pull it into a sleek ponytail, or curl the ends. Put some lipstick on. Spritz some perfume. It might feel absurd, but just do it anyway. You might garner a lot of attention the first few times you do this. *"Where are you going?"* *"Wow, someone dressed up today!"* Just accept the comments with a smile. Keep pushing yourself to do this on a daily basis. No matter what you have planned for the day, present yourself beautifully. There's no need to become a high-maintenance diva, spending an hour in the bathroom getting ready. Just put some thought and, yes, bravery into your outfit and toilette. After a while it will become the new standard you hold yourself to, and it will feel foreign and uncomfortable to be in your frumpy old sweatpants again.

Embracing your femininity is a marvelous way to celebrate being a woman. You don't need to do it for anyone other than yourself. Each and every woman is beautiful and unique in her own way. We are all one of a kind. Let us honor that on a daily basis. And even though you are only doing this for yourself, it will have positive effects on everyone in your life. Your children will have wonderful memories of a mom who was vibrant and beautiful, not frumpy and overwhelmed. Your husband will appreciate the effort and might up his game a little too. Your friends will be inspired. Looking presentable will always have a ripple effect in your life that will touch others in the most unexpected ways.

Cultivate Your Signature Look

Just as you can have a signature perfume and a signature drink (which we'll discuss soon), you can have a signature look. A woman in Paris I call Madame Bohemienne always wore sleeveless or three-quarter-sleeve knit tops and flowing skirts. Madame Chic always wore classic A-line skirts and sweater sets or silk blouses. This is not to say they weren't fashionable because they wore the same look all the time. They just knew what they liked. I'm sure that when it came time for Madame Bohemienne to update her wardrobe and she came across a beautiful bohemian-like flowing skirt, she would buy it. She was a connoisseur of her own look and had an eye for what was quintessentially her. This is why both women looked so comfortable in their own skins. They weren't hiding their styles by wearing exercise clothes all day long. They weren't trying to keep up with the trends. They dressed purely for themselves and wore what flattered them and made them happy.

When I release my ten-item wardrobe videos on YouTube, many viewers comment that the looks are so me. I love to hear that, because that's what I'm going for! I am not trying to be a fashionista on the cutting edge of trends. I'm trying to be Jennifer Scott: stay-at-home mom, writer, and housewife. I am aiming to be comfortable yet stylish every day. I'm aiming to journey through life looking presentable and adding beauty to the world. I am a connoisseur of my own style.

Now that you have embraced the ten-item capsule wardrobe, or some variation of it, and have carefully curated your extras (T-shirts, blazers, coats, special-occasion dresses, blouses, and accessories), you will have clarity when you decide upon your signature look. What will you be known for? What are you most comfortable in? (And exercise clothes are not the answer.) Do you have at least three signature looks you can pin down?

I have a few signature looks I just can't quit. And why would I want to? They are so me, and I love them. One signature look is the blazer, T-shirt, skinny-jean, and ballet-flat combination. In this outfit I can run errands and still look very pulled together. When I'm shopping for blazers, I like to choose those with interest: a velvet blazer or a knit tweed blazer. This adds variety to my look and I don't get bored with it. I'll wear ballet flats with interesting textures like faux ostrich or faux croc. Or I'll find shoes in unique colors like deep plum or emerald rather than the usual gray and black.

My second signature look is the skinny jean and nautical tee. No matter what the season is, I always have one or two (or three) nautical-inspired T-shirts. Some are the traditional Breton navy-striped fisherman tees (so Coco Chanel) and some are a twist on the classic: a periwinkle-blue-and-white-striped boat-neck tee, for example, still has nautical influence but is a bit modernized. I'll wear this look with white jeans and patent nude sandals in the summer, dark-wash jeans and driving loafers in the fall, and with riding boots and wool trench coat in the winter.

My third signature look is the dress. A dress is a complete look all its own; I don't have to work hard to try and make it go with anything. I tend to like knee-length dresses—more flowy ones in the summer, and more structured ones in the winter. I always have a wrap dress on hand.

So, you see, with these three beloved signature looks of mine, I never have one of those days where I don't know what to wear. If I do, I simply default to one of my favorites and am always happy in it.

Let's say one of your signature looks is a flowy dress and cardigan. You always feel great when you wear this combination. Whenever you go shopping to update your wardrobe, you keep your eye out for the most exquisite silk dress you can find—in the most flattering colors for your skin tone. You love plums, for example, and you see a beautiful strappy number that is just perfect for a warm spring day. It is made of gorgeous purple hues with flecks of green and gray. It pairs so nicely with that green cashmere cardigan you purchased last winter. Voilà, another fabulous addition to your wardrobe, another variation on your signature look that will help you feel beautiful, comfortable, and presentable. Become a connoisseur of your own look, and picking out your clothes in the morning will be such a joy.

Assess your signature look regularly and make sure you're keeping it modern. You don't want to end up on a makeover show because your loved ones worry you're trapped in the eighties. Consult a stylist or a fashionable friend whose opinion you trust. Have fun cultivating these looks. They are your fashionable stamp on the world.

Chic Tip

Enjoy the secret details of dressing every day. Don't wear your granny panties and hole-y socks (in fact, throw them away). Pick out a beautiful matching bra and panty set to wear today. Yes, today! Even though you don't have a hot date. Even though no one will see them. You will know you are wearing them, and that is enough. Wear your nice lingerie and spritz yourself with your favorite fragrance. Then put your clothes on. Enjoy these secret details. You'll have a decided spring in your step throughout your hectic day.

◦ Morning Beauty Routine ◦

My number one skin-care tip is to not overcleanse your skin. We are too harsh on our skin—always scrubbing, cleansing, and exfoliating it. We don't allow our natural oils to cultivate, and because of this our skin works overtime producing even more oil. Because I'd like to avoid this, generally my morning beauty routine is quite simple: I splash some warm water on my face and moisturize with a day cream that has an SPF.

That's it! How wonderful that you don't need to do an entire cleansing regimen in the morning. Use the extra time to do your hair and makeup or simply enjoy your coffee for a few moments longer.

I love to do my makeup. It brings me joy. Some days I get further than others. Many days all I wear is spot concealer (if needed), eyebrow powder (I always fill in my eyebrows because they are so sparse), and mascara. This is my one-minute look for days when I want my skin to breathe or I simply don't have time to do a more elaborate routine. When I do have an extra five to seven minutes in the morning, I have great fun figuring out what I want to do with my makeup for the day. Here are three basic looks that I enjoy wearing daily:

Chic Parisian Look

Apply foundation, under-eye concealer, and spot concealer. Set with powder. Fill in the eyebrows lightly with powder. After applying eye shadow primer, sweep a soft pink, (barely) shimmery shadow over the entire lid. With a clean eyeliner brush, apply gel liner (one of my favorites is Bobbi Brown

Long-Wear Gel Eyeliner in Caviar Ink). Start with a thin line at the inward corner of the eye, then build the line thicker as you move toward the end of the eye. Apply a barely there pink blush on the apples of your cheeks. Apply mascara. Apply lip balm and, if desired, a sweep of pale pink lipstick. Voilà!

California Chic

Apply tinted moisturizer or BB cream with SPF. Apply a highlight concealer to brighten the under-eye area. If needed, apply spot concealer. Set with powder only under the eyes, on the forehead, nose, and chin, leaving the cheeks alone. Fill in the eyebrows with a subtle powder. Apply several coats of mascara to the lashes to make the eyes stand out. Apply a bronzer in an E shape, touching the temples, cheekbones, and under the jawline. Blend. Apply a cream blush, if desired. Apply lip balm or a sheer lip gloss. You are now a sun-kissed California girl.

London Chic

Apply under-eye concealer. Sweep on a liquid foundation or a mineral powder foundation. Spot conceal if necessary. Fill in eyebrows with a powder. Apply eye shadow primer. Sweep a light neutral powder (nothing too shimmery) on the lid. Apply a light taupe color to the crease of the eyelid. Blend. With a brush, apply gel liner to the top eyelid, being sure to keep as close to the lid as possible. With a kohl pencil liner, line the waterline of the lower eyelid. Apply mascara to top and bottom lashes. Apply a rose-colored blush to the apples of the cheeks. Apply a creamy pale-rose lipstick or lip balm. Behold the English Rose.

Get inspired by beautiful women all around the globe. Use a smoky kohl liner all around the eyes for a sultry Middle Eastern look. Go for a classic Italian cat-eye look by practicing a wingtip (think Sophia Loren). In fact, look at your favorite film stars and see how they wear their makeup. Have fun trying to emulate their looks and custom-tailoring them to colors that flatter your complexion. Make your daily routine of applying makeup joyful. I like to think of the whole process as a wonderful, creative experience.

～ Hair ～

When you have a moment, practice some hairdos that only take a few minutes and will help you look polished and pulled together. After some practice, you can perfect your favorite 'dos and achieve them in no time at all. Here are a few of my favorite hair looks:

Half-up/Half-down Variations

Bohemian braids

Section off a small amount of hair on either side of your part. Take one section and create a loose braid. Make sure you pull the braid back as you braid so that when you pin it up, it conforms to the shape of your head. Repeat on the other side. Take the two braids back until they meet in the middle of the back of your head. Cross one over the other. Then hide the ends by tucking them into the braided section. Pin with bobby pins. Set with hair spray, if desired. This bohemian look is perfect to wear on a glorious summer day.

Retro

Brush the hair through with a boar bristle brush to create smooth, yet voluminous hair. With a rattail comb, tease the hair on the crown of the head (spray this section with hair spray first for a stronger hold). Smooth over with a brush, without taking any of the volume out. Take two sections of hair on either side and pull them back to meet in the middle of the back of your head. Twist one section over the other. Push up slightly to increase the volume at the crown of your head. Pin into place. Set with hair spray, if desired. This look is wonderful for anytime you'd like to look polished and *très* chic.

Chignon

Sixties chignon

I learned this look from YouTube sensation Sara Sabaté. Brush your hair with a boar-bristle brush to make it smooth and voluminous. Section the hair half-up and half-down. Secure the top half of hair on top of your head with a clip, just to get it out of the way. Wrap a hair band around the bottom half of the hair to create a low ponytail. Pull the hair band halfway down the ponytail. Then take the bottom of the ponytail and roll it under until you have reached the base of your head and have hidden the hair tie. Secure underneath with bobby pins. Then release the top half of hair. Tease the hair at the crown of the head with a rattail comb. Brush smooth, without releasing the volume you have just created. Then, just as with the retro half-up/half-down look described above, pin the hair back by taking sections on either side of the head and pinning in the middle as the hair meets at the back of the head. Take the remainder of hair and now pin under everything (under where you pinned the rolled-up hair with the hair tie). Secure with hair spray. This is a great ladylike hairstyle. Use eyeliner to create a cat-eye style for the ultimate retro look.

Low-swept side chignon

Fabulous hairstylist Natasha Sunshine showed me this ten-second updo. Pull your hair into a low side ponytail, keeping the hair on the crown of the head loose (this is an artfully messy look; don't pull too tight). Secure with an elastic band. Take another elastic band and tie it around the hair at the bottom of the ponytail. Now take a few strands of hair with your fingers and push up the rest of the hair. This will now look like a messy bun with a tail sticking out of it. Take the "tail" and wrap it across the bun, tucking it behind. Secure the whole look with four or five bobby pins. Set with hair spray. This look is wonderfully romantic and versatile. It's fancy enough for a formal event and also looks pretty with a casual spring day dress.

Buns

Messy bun

Brush your hair into a high ponytail atop your head. Secure the ponytail with an elastic band. Loosely wrap the hair around in a clockwise fashion. It's okay if strands are loose and the bun is messy (that is what we are going for, after all). Secure the base of the bun with several bobby pins. Set with hair spray. The messy bun is great to wear when you haven't washed your hair for a day (or two) and it doesn't look presentable down.

Chic bun

Create a deep side part in your hair and brush with a boar bristle brush to smooth. Gather your hair into a low ponytail at the base of your head. Tie with a hair band. Wrap your hair around the base of the ponytail until your bun is complete. Secure with another elastic, if desired, or simply with bobby pins. Spray down any flyaways with hair spray.

Sock bun

Create your own sock bun out of a pair of (clean) socks that match your hair color. Cut the toes off the socks and roll until you get a doughnut shape. Or, if you're like me and feel a bit weird about wearing a real sock on your head, you can buy a hair doughnut from the drugstore or beauty store for around three dollars. Create a ponytail and secure with an elastic. Then thread the hair at the end of the ponytail through the sock bun. Roll it down toward the base of the pony-tail in an outward fashion, making sure the hair is evenly distributed around the bun. When it reaches your head, secure with pins, if necessary. Place your ponytail wherever you'd like to create different effects. Place the ponytail (and subsequent bun) at the top of your head for a Sarah Jessica Parker–*Sex and the City* look. Wear a low, side bun for a more romantic look. For a ballet look, keep the hair sleek and place it on the back of your head between the ears. Have fun with this!

Ponytail

The sleek ponytail

Use a natural boar bristle brush to brush your hair back and up into the desired location of your ponytail. Wrap with a hair tie. Take a few strands of hair from the bot-tom of the ponytail and wrap around the base of the ponytail to conceal the hair tie. Pin in place with one or two bobby pins. If desired, set with hair spray. The sleek ponytail is a marvelous, everyday look and is wonderful for when you are doing a lot of housework and don't want your hair to get in the way.

The chic ponytail

Create a side part in your hair. Tease the hair at the crown of the head with a rattail comb. Smooth with a boar bristle brush, but without reducing the volume you just created. Pull your hair into a low ponytail at the base of the head. Secure with a hair tie. As with the sleek ponytail described above, take a few strands of hair from underneath the ponytail and wrap around the hair tie in order to conceal it. Secure with one or two bobby pins. Set with hair spray. This ponytail has a marvelous Audrey Hepburn–*Breakfast at Tiffany's* look to it.

The bad-hair-day ponytail

Run a boar bristle brush through your hair to smooth it out as much as possible. Pull your hair into a pony-tail centered in the back of your head. Secure with an elastic. Conceal the elastic with a small strand of hair and secure with a bobby pin. Place a thin black wrap-around headband around your head, sitting around one inch away from the hairline. This headband (they make fabulous ones now that look like ribbons) will tame any bad-hair-day flyaways and will make even the messiest ponytail look chic and high fashion.

These are just a few of the hairstyles I do on a regular basis. Because I wash my hair every third (or sometimes fourth) day, I usually wear my hair down for the first two days. The next day I wear one of the above updos. Practice these styles when you have some time so that each morning you can pick a look, pull it off, and look fabulous. For more hair tutorials, check out my YouTube channel, The Daily Connoisseur.

 Grooming

It is not necessary to have a big grooming session in the morning—this is better saved for evenings, when you have more time—but it is important to check your grooming before you go out for the day. Did that dry shampoo disappear completely in your hair, or do you look like an extra from *Amadeus*? Do you have any jagged or dirty nails? Chipped nail polish? Lipstick on your teeth? Any hairs you'd like to get rid of quickly?

One day I was looking at my makeup in the magnifying mirror. I happened to look down toward my *décolleté* and noticed a hair that had fallen on my chest. I brushed it aside with my hand but it didn't move. I brushed it again. *Move!* I thought. It did not move. That's when I realized it was attached to my chest. Ack! I had a chest hair! I wondered how long it had been there. How many people had seen my chest hair? *Why did I have a chest hair?* Needless to say, I plucked that pesky thing and now regularly check to see if it has returned. Don't judge.

Have a look at yourself in a hand mirror in natural light. See yourself how other people see you. Is your makeup blended well? You know it is if you can't tell you're wearing any at all. That is the goal. No one should notice your foundation. Check your hair as well to make sure any product you've used is blended in. Great. Now, before leaving the house, make sure to wipe those stray dog or cat hairs off your sweater with your lint brush. Your morning grooming session is complete.

Getting Ready: Chic Tips for Working Women
....

Preparation is of the utmost importance if you are going to experience a smooth morning before heading out to work. With the right amount of preparation, you can glide through your morning and actually enjoy it.

- *Pack your briefcase and tote the night before. While you're there, make sure to clear out any clutter, such as old receipts, tissues, and loose change.*

- *In the evening, lay out the clothes you will wear the following day, right down to the corresponding accessories, so you are not pulling out the contents of your lingerie drawer to search for the right shade of tights in the morning rush. I know a chic working woman who keeps her stockings in separate bags according to color so she's not trying to figure out which is blue and which is black in the dim morning light. This would come in handy if you forgot to lay your clothes out the night before.*

- *Plan what you are going to have for breakfast the night before and set out any necessary ingredients (keep the re-*

frigerated food together, set dry ingredients on the counter-top). Blend your morning smoothie drink and keep it in the fridge ready for the next morning. Set the timer on your coffee machine so you awaken to the fresh aroma of your favorite brew.

- I still advocate sitting down to eat breakfast, but on those mornings when you are running late for the train, you can always put that smoothie in a to-go cup or thermos.

- If you are taking the kids to day care on the way to work, make sure everything is packed. Lay out their clothes for the day, keep the sunscreen accessible, and pack any snacks and water bottles that might be needed. Keep this all by the front door so you don't forget anything.

MUSIC FOR THE MORNING COMMUTE

Mozart for the Morning Commute: A Lively Bit of Traveling Music (compilation), Philips, 1997.

This exuberant collection of songs will negate any travel-related frustrations and have you ready to start the working day refreshed.

The Tantalizing Tangos of Argentina by Buenos Aires Tango Orchestra, Legacy, 1999.

Add some passion to your morning commute with the sultry sounds of the Argentinian tango.

I Love Paris! Classic Gypsy Swing & French Accordion Jazz by Café Chill Lounge Club, Warner/Chappell Production Music, 2012.

Envision yourself riding a bicycle to work on Paris's cobblestone streets, your scarf waving artistically behind you.

Putumayo Presents: Italian Café (compilation), Putumayo World Music, 2005.

Take your commute in style as these classic Italian songs serenade you.

Club de Paris: Traditional French Café Music by Café Chill Lounge Club, Warner/Chappell Production Music, 2012.

Escape the neck-to-neck traffic by immersing yourself in traditional Parisian café music.

Putumayo Presents: Cuba (compilation), Putumayo World Music, 1999.

Sway all the way to the office as you listen to the exotic sounds of Cuban *son* music.

 Kids

There are a million variations on the morning routine with children. Only you know what needs to get done. As I have small children, I'm relatively new to all of this, but one thing that is very important to me is to not create an atmosphere of rushing but, rather, one of calm.

We are our children's first teachers. They mimic everything we do. Last night I was dancing with my girls after dinner. We were parading around the dining room table with our bells and shakers dancing to Mumford & Sons (random, I know). I was leading this conga line and they were happily trailing behind me. I stopped for a second to adjust my hair—my bun had started to fall out. My fifteen-month-old, thinking this was a dance move, stopped and started to fiddle with her hair. I finished and started dancing again. My daughters did too, but for the rest of the song, the baby stopped every few seconds to do the new dance move she'd learned: "fix her hair."

I want our mornings to be full of pleasure. I want my children to wake up wide-eyed in anticipation of the excitement of the day. It is important for them to know their routines and what they have to get done in a timely manner, but I don't want them to rush through their routines. I want them to enjoy them. Ralph Waldo Emerson's words "Life is a journey, not a destination" bear repeating here. The destination is school, but the journey to get there should be pleasant too. Life is in the present moment. We are not at school yet: we are eating breakfast, brushing our teeth, and getting our shoes on. The goal is to do all of this with awareness. Anxiety is caused by thinking about the future. It is my job to keep an eye on the time and to not be late for school. If you find that your kids are always late for school, try to move up their wake-up time so you can get everything done that needs to get done without anxiety or rushing.

Sometimes we will rush just because it's what we think we're supposed to be doing. When my older daughter first started preschool, I would rush her out the door, holding her little hand as we power walked to school. We would sing the White Rabbit's song from *Alice in Wonderland*. After doing this three days in a row, I realized what I was doing. I was making my daughter anxious that we would be late for school and that there would be awful consequences. It was a negative approach to going to school, not a positive one. We stopped singing that song. Now we walk slowly, if we feel like it. She has time to pick up as many pinecones as she likes. We occasionally see Mr. Squirrel and Mr. Crow. She likes to pick wildflowers and bring them to her teachers. When we get to the classroom, they put the flowers in a mini vase on the children's lunch table. And guess what? We haven't been late yet. Life is beautiful, and if we were rushing to school every day, we would miss all of that magic—the flowers, the squirrels, the fresh crisp air—all of it. And what a shame it would be to miss that.

Chic Tip: Nagging and How to Avoid It

Every woman has caught herself doing this. We swore we would never do it. Nagging. The definition of "nag," according to the dictionary, is to "annoy or irritate (a person) with persistent fault-finding or continuous urging." We nag our husbands. We nag our children. I've done it. You've most likely done it. It can be so hard not to do it. We run the home, after all. We ask people to do things, and they simply don't do them!

In his book The Four Agreements, *Miguel Ruiz says the most important agreement is the first: be impeccable with your word. Nagging is not being impeccable with your word. It could be that the nagging has gotten out of hand and your family members tune you out. (As always,*

I speak from experience.) Try being impeccable with your word. Ask calmly and nicely the first time. It might not get done today, or even for a long while. But when you get into the powerful habit of asking something in a clear voice, with uncharged undertones (no negative connotations at all), over time a miracle will occur.

I used to nag my kids to wash their hands when they got home. I tried everything. I would chase them around the house. I would tell them they'd get a cold if they didn't wash the germs off. Please? Come on! I would dance around like a monkey trying to get them to go wash their hands. None of this ever worked. My daughter would sense my desperation and capitalize on it. She acted like it was a game of hide-and-seek and would deliberately run away. I was nagging her, and neither of us liked it. Then I tried something else. Every day when we got home, I would say, "Let's go wash our hands." There was no charge behind it. I said it with calm, loving authority.

She looked at me and asked, "Why?"

"Because it's nice to have clean hands at home and clean hands help to keep us healthy."

"Okay, Mommy," she said. She's strayed a few times,

but now it's become a habit. Not a fear-based habit—I don't want her to wash her hands because she's afraid of catching a cold. I tried to turn it into a positive habit: it is nice for our hands to be clean at home.

Signature Drink

James Bond liked his vodka martini shaken, not stirred. Precious Ramotswe drinks her rooibos tea without milk and sugar. Hercule Poirot insists upon taking his tisane in the proper glass cup. Any other way, and it simply wouldn't be the same.

I'm sure you have one too, a drink that—no matter how special or ordinary—you enjoy having every day. It could be a cup of strong black coffee every morning or your morning cup of tea. The variation and variety might change, but with regularity you enjoy the same beverage.

In my high school drama class, we did a Stanislavski exercise where we sat with an imaginary hot cup of coffee and mimed how we would drink it. Most of the actors did the same thing when it was their turn to mime. We sat in the chair with our hands around the imaginary mug of coffee. We closed our eyes and inhaled the scent of the "coffee." Then we took a sip and sat back and savored. We took deep breaths. We would do the exercise for a whole minute. These were some dramatic coffee drinking sessions! The purpose of the acting exercise was to get in the space of everyday life, exploring the realistic nuances of the moment and getting comfortable with just being.

Now that I think about it, I'm not sure how realistic we were as actors. If I wanted an A-plus in that acting exercise, I really should have had the coffee in my hand while running around the room, yelling at the kids with the phone at my ear, trying to talk to customer service about a late bill payment. The reality is that we are usually so rushed, we sip our signature drink between tasks, running around the house to get ready or even driving on the way to work. Wouldn't it be nice if we took a little more time with our signature drink? If you get a moment, sit down with your signature drink and, as in the Stanislavski exercise (but this time for real), savor it. Feel its warmth (or coolness) on your hands. Inhale its lovely aroma. Imagine it to be a magic elixir that gives you energy for the rest of the day.

When traveling, it's nice to embrace the signature drink

of the country you're visiting. In Paris, I would have a warm bowl (yes, bowl) of tea with Madame Chic: black tea, no milk. In England, we always have English breakfast tea with milk and sugar. In Sri Lanka, when staying with my friend Anjali's family, we would have black tea with sweetened condensed milk. When in Rome (yes), we would have cappuccinos. Back in California, when I do my writing at Caffe Luxxe, the same people saunter in every morning to have their signature drink. At Caffe Luxxe I stick with my Roman cappuccino. The employees pretty much all know the regulars' "usual."

My signature drink has changed over the years. I used to drink green tea exclusively until I became pregnant with my first child. It isn't advised to drink green tea during pregnancy and nursing, so I switched to Mma Ramotswe's favorite rooibos tea. Now that that phase of life is over, I have the opportunity to choose a new signature drink. I have been a bit indecisive of late, as I try different blends and variations on my favorite teas. I'm enjoying this process immensely, though, and that is the point of all of this, isn't it?

Here are some unusual recipes for when you'd like to try out a new signature drink.

Rooibos Tea Latte

Mma Ramotswe (from the No. 1 Ladies' Detective Agency books) would not approve of this drink, as she prefers her rooibos without embellishment, but I sure get a kick out of this version.

Almost boiling water

Loose leaf rooibos tea (1 heaping teaspoon per person)

Soy, almond, or hemp milk, warmed

Honey or stevia (if you like it sweet)

In a kettle, get your water to almost boiling, then pour into a teapot. Spoon in your rooibos tea proportionate to how many people will be drinking it. Let it steep for five minutes. Pour the tea into cups, using a strainer to keep the tea leaves out of your cup. Pour in your warm milk of choice (my favorite with this is almond milk). If using sweetener, add it here. Use a frothing stick to froth to a delightfully effervescent texture. Enjoy. (Check out my Rooibos Tea Latte tutorial on YouTube for a visual guide to making this lovely drink.)

Chai Tea Latte for One

I often have this in the autumn months.

Take 1 tea bag of Assam (black) tea, or a small spoonful of loose tea leaves. Place it in a small pan with 1 cup of water, half a cinnamon stick (those things are expensive, so cut it in half), a pinch of cardamom, a pinch of ground ginger, and 1 clove. Boil for 2–3 minutes. Then add a cup of almond milk (or whatever milk you prefer) and a teaspoon of sugar. Bring to a boil again. Pour through a strainer into a mug. Enjoy!

Chai Tea Latte for Two or Three People

2 cups water

2 black tea bags or 2 heaping teaspoons of loose leaf black tea

⅛ teaspoon each of ground ginger and cardamom

1 cinnamon stick

1 whole clove

Up to ¼ cup of sugar (depending on how sweet you like it) or 2 tablespoons honey or a packet of stevia

2½ cups of almond, soy, or cow's milk (I like to use Califia Farms's Coconut Almond Milk)

Add the water, tea, and spices to a saucepan. Bring to a boil for 5 minutes. Add sugar. Add milk and return to a boil (but don't let it boil over). Strain into teacups and enjoy.

....

My Ultimate Signature Drink

Yes, I know this is a bit cheeky. And don't laugh. But if I had to pin down one signature drink that I would have forever, it would be warm water with lemon. I have this every single morning when I wake up. I walk to the kitchen, get my glass, and fill it with half hot water and half cold water (from our water dispenser). I cut a lemon in half and squeeze (I never throw the lemon half away. I use it by either cutting it up and putting it down the garbage disposal to rid it of odor, or I place it in the dishwasher, impaled on one of the prongs. This freshens up the dishes). This drink will loosen up any toxins you have in your system, and it does wonders for the skin.

◦ Breakfast ◦

I like to think of breakfast as the opening act of the play that is our day. And no matter how small or how grand, it should be relished and enjoyed. Pay attention to how you are nourishing your body, and realize that by doing so you are setting yourself up to thrive for the rest of the day.

Breakfast should ideally be organized the night before. This includes deciding what to eat as well as setting the table. (This will be addressed further in the evening section.) Knowing what's for breakfast can entice you to get up in the morning. Think seasonally here. In the summer you will want lighter fare than in the winter. But whether you are having Greek yogurt with berries or hot oatmeal with raisins, almond milk, and toasted coconut, take your time.

Breakfast is so often rushed through. It's really nice, for a change, to put music on, open the window, and sit down, even for only five minutes, and enjoy your food. If you don't want to listen to music, put talk radio on, or don't listen to anything at all. Just be with your food and enjoy it. I get that for many mothers this is virtually impossible. I find myself preparing breakfast for everyone, including the dog, while walking around sipping my own liquid breakfast. So I understand that sitting down isn't always possible. But every morning I do try to sit down with my kids, even if only for two minutes, to connect with them. I surrender. Breakfast is the opening act of the play. It's when you really get into the flow of the day. It should be as rapturous as possible. Yes, as rapturous as a Tuesday morning will allow.

After reading Kimberly Snyder's *The Beauty Detox Solution*, I have enjoyed making her glowing green smoothie for breakfast. I often put my own spin on it, but I love drinking this in the morning. I might have other things to eat with it, or I might not, but it feels magnificent to drink so many green vegetables in the morning. Okay, I realize that sounds highly unappetizing, but try it! Also, you won't believe this, but my daughters really love their "smoothie drink," and I have marvelous peace of mind knowing they are getting so many vegetables in at the beginning of the day. Here is my take on the recipe:

Green Smoothie

1 cup water

3 stalks celery, chopped (if you don't have celery, you can still
make this, just add more spinach)

1 pear or apple, chopped

1 banana (put in a frozen banana for a milk shake
consistency, or if you're out of fresh bananas)

Half a head of lettuce (butter, romaine, or the spring mix from
the grocery store. Avoid arugula, herb lettuce mixes, or
iceberg lettuce)

Two handfuls chopped spinach or chopped kale (if you don't
have spinach, use a whole head of lettuce. If you don't
have lettuce, use only spinach)

One packet of stevia

Put it all in the blender and blend till smooth. Delicious.

....

This makes enough for me and the girls for two days (my
husband has not hopped on the green smoothie bandwagon
with us . . . yet). If I know the morning is going to be hectic,

I will make this the night before, pour into individual glasses, cover with plastic wrap, and store in the refrigerator. Just stir the smoothie before you drink it the following morning.

When we are in the mood for a sweeter and creamier breakfast drink, I love to make this green shake that gives you lots of energy thanks to the almond butter and greens powder. This shake has a light green hue and is mild, creamy, sweet, and satisfying all at the same time.

Morning Green Shake

1½ cups almond milk (or coconut almond milk)

1 serving greens powder (a wide variety can be found at a health food store)

1 large ripe banana

1 heaping tablespoon almond butter

2 teaspoons raw honey

Place all ingredients in a blender and mix until smooth. Serves 2.

. . . .

I have a smoothie drink probably five days a week. I think it does wonders for my skin and my health. If I need heartier fare, I also have a piece of crispy, buttery toast drizzled with raw honey. Or I'll have more fruit. Or I'll have oatmeal. It just depends on what I feel like. I listen to my body to see what it wants. We usually have pancakes or waffles on Saturday and bacon and eggs (turkey bacon for me, *merci*) on Sunday. The girls love lots of fruit, cheese, yogurt, their green smoothie, whole-grain toast, or oatmeal. Not all together, mind you, but they pick and choose. They love breakfast so much that they often call other meals of the day "breakfast." I want them to enjoy and be passionate about food. So this makes me happy.

I still remember breakfast with Madame Chic. Every morning I enjoyed traipsing down the hall to that charming little kitchen to start the day eating delightful treats: a tartine with homemade jam, a slice of last night's tart, a yogurt or *petit-suisse* all washed down with a bowl of tea. There was no guilt eating this breakfast, only pleasure. Listening to the tinkling sound of the radio, with the open window allowing the cool Parisian air to flow in. That's what breakfast is all about. Nourishing yourself, preparing for the day ahead, and enjoying every minute of it.

Chic Tip

It is a great thing to be on top of current events and know what is going on in the world, but be careful that you don't obsess and internalize all of the negative news of the day. Practice processing it without allowing yourself to be manipulated. Be informed, but be aware of how the media often use fear tactics to grip readers. While you are reading, try to filter out the spin and see the information for what it is. If a situation is upsetting you and causing you to live your life in fear, take a few deep breaths and bring yourself to the present moment. Right in this very moment, you are okay. If you can do something today to help the situation, do it. If not, try to send the situation love and move on with your day.

Elevenses

For special mornings when you have a little extra time, it can be fun to have friends over for elevenses. Elevenses is traditionally a social gathering that takes place around eleven a.m. (hence the name). It has currently gone out of vogue, but I think that is such a shame. Paddington Bear and Mr. Gruber had elevenses, and look what fun they had! At elevenses, coffee is typically served along with a breakfast cake. Paddington's choice is toast with marmalade and butter. My preference is coffee cake. What is your preference?

How wonderful to invite a friend or two over and have a chat over cake and a cup of tea or coffee. A homemade cake would be ideal but isn't totally necessary. When I make break-fast cakes, I like to double the batch and freeze a cake for last-minute elevenses. As always, think seasonally. You could make pumpkin bread in the fall and zucchini bread in the spring. Or almond cake in the winter and lemon cake in the summer. But, of course, nothing beats a traditional coffee cake.

Sour Cream Coffee Bundt Cake

flour-coated baking spray

1 cup butter, room temperature

2 cups sugar

2 eggs

1 cup sour cream

½ teaspoon vanilla extract

Sift together:

2 cups all-purpose flour

1 teaspoon baking powder

⅛ teaspoon salt

Filling:

⅓ cup all-purpose flour

½ cup packed brown sugar

2 tablespoons melted butter

1 teaspoon ground cinnamon

Preheat the oven to 350 degrees F. Spray a bundt pan with flour-coated baking spray. In a large bowl, cream together 1 cup butter and the sugar until light and fluffy. Beat in the eggs one at a time, then stir in the sour cream and vanilla. Mix in 2 cups flour, baking powder, and salt.

To prepare the filling: in a medium bowl mix ⅓ cup flour, brown sugar, 2 tablespoons melted butter, and cinnamon.

Pour half of the batter into the pan. Sprinkle the brown sugar filling evenly over the batter. Pour the rest of the batter on top of the filling.

Bake 40–45 minutes or until a toothpick inserted in the thickest part of the cake comes out clean.

. . . .

Elevenses does not have to be fancy. It should be charming and intimate. Set a cozy table with a patterned tablecloth and have cloth napkins ready. Or set out a tray on the ottoman by the fire. If it's a warm day, go sit outside. Get out your best teacups for tea or mugs for coffee. Make sure your drinks are piping hot and the cake warm from the oven. If you baked the cake the day before, pop it in the oven for ten minutes at 300 degrees F to warm it up. Serve the cake, sip from your warm mugs of coffee, and have a lovely chat. What a wonderful way to treat yourself every now and then and celebrate the day.

⌒⊙ Brunch ⊙⌒

Brunch, like elevenses and afternoon tea, is a great, low-stress way to entertain your friends. You do not have to worry about the formalities of a sit-down dinner party. The food can all be prepared beforehand and set out, buffet style, allowing you to enjoy your guests.

The key to a great brunch spread is abundance. You don't have to prepare dozens of dishes, but make what you do prepare appear bountiful. Here are some ideas:

- A bowl full of enticing bagels (lay a cloth in the bowl before adding the bagels and allow the edges of the cloth to hang over the side of the bowl)

- A pretty platter with artfully arranged sliced tomatoes, capers, sliced red onions, and lox

- A little dish with cream cheese and a unique serving knife

- A bowl of fruit salad

- A savory breakfast casserole

- Croissants or *pain au chocolat*

- Quiche (caramelized onion, spinach, broccoli, or whatever your favorite is)

- Assorted salads

- Sparkling water

- Juice

- A signature brunch cocktail like mango mimosas (sparkling wine with a splash of mango juice)

- Assortment of teas and coffee

These are just some suggestions. Pick one or two, or pick them all. Make the table look enticing. Lay down a beautiful tablecloth. Mix and match your serving dishes and utensils. Include a bouquet of flowers. Your guests will be so pleased. Play some lively music in the background. Brunch should be festive.

Yohan and Barbara, our Parisian friends in California, put on a smashing brunch. They said they discovered brunch when they moved to America—that in Paris it's not quite done. But true to form, they took on the celebration and perfected it in their own special way. And now they are connoisseurs of brunch—which makes us very happy as guests when we come to visit! Barbara bakes a few homemade quiches and always has a stack of freshly made crepes next to a pot of chocolate hazelnut spread. A fruit salad and vegetable salad are always available. They serve up a delicious cappuccino. Their brunch spread is beautiful in its simplicity.

I recently went out to brunch at a local Santa Monica restaurant with my parents, who were visiting. The restaurant had it just right. The menu was varied and abundant, and the cocktails flowed. A DJ was playing lively music. We had so much fun! It felt like a party on a late Sunday morning. We took our older daughter with us, and she loved it. We were all dancing in our seats. Create a similarly carefree atmosphere. If you have an outdoor space, use it and brunch al fresco.

∽ Putting Things Away ∾

Inevitably after any morning, hectic or not, there will be things to put away. The key is to try to put them away when you are finished using them, not to save the cleanup for later. This will diminish the mess you have to clear up at the end of the day. Before preparing a meal, I like to start with a clean kitchen so that the tidying-up process afterward is relatively quick. It is the same principle we teach our children but don't always follow ourselves (hello! I'm guilty)—that when you take something out, put it away when you are finished with it. This applies to everything from the sugar to the coffee grounds to last night's pajamas to your makeup brushes.

It sounds simple and hardly worth repeating, but you would be surprised how many people, in their rush, leave things out, contributing to the all-over feeling of chaos and clutter. In reality, completing the task and putting your things away only takes a few extra seconds. These few extra seconds save you time and aggravation later.

Rather than thinking about it as a chore, incorporate the cleanup into the flow of the day. The usual energy of the morning is bubbling and filled with excitement. Use that energy. You might as well tackle it with a positive attitude. Sing while you do it. Dance while you do it. Choose to be happy with what you are doing now.

⌒∘ Exercise ∘⌒

Power yoga might be your thing. Or maybe you like to run a few times a week. Whatever form of exercise you think you do, there's another kind you might be overlooking. It's in every part of your active day. Suddenly the prospect of cleaning the house or vacuuming the stairs doesn't seem so unappealing when you realize that you are also getting vital exercise in.

This simple shift in perception can make your life so much easier. Do you see the glass half-empty, or do you see it half-full? If you have to lug the heavy water bottles up two flights of stairs when they are delivered (my chore), are you cursing the stairs, the water bottles, and the whole situation in general? Or are you looking at it as a way to fit exercise into your day?

In fact, bringing in the water bottles is great strength resistance training. It tones my arms and makes me focus on my breathing. It's good abdominal work when I lift the water bottle into the dispenser. Whenever the water bottles are delivered, I know I'm going to get some extra exercise that day.

Some people ask me how I've managed to shed the weight after having two babies. It's because I have a very active day every day. Even today I challenged myself physically, but I had to actively seek it out. I parked my car on the seventh floor of a parking structure. Not wanting to wait for the elevator, I walked down seven flights of stairs. On the way back I made the split-second decision to not hop into the open elevator that was awaiting me. I decided to walk. I power walked up those seven flights of stairs. Around the fifth flight I really started to feel the burn. It was a good burn. I was completely out of breath when I reached my car, but I took a moment, along with a large swig of water, and felt invigorated. Enough with a sedentary life. I like pumping oxygen into my veins whenever I can.

Exercise is a part of life, not a chore. That is my philosophy now. If you can walk instead of drive, walk. If you have to vacuum the carpet, do it with relish. It's exercise. It all is. Just because it's not taking place while you're wearing leggings in the gym doesn't mean it isn't valid.

Chic Exercise Clothes

When you are working out, devote the same philosophy to your exercise clothes that you would to your regular clothes. This doesn't mean you have to wear the trendiest and most expensive gear, but that you wear an outfit that flatters your figure and makes you feel good about exercising. Some people just wear oversized sweats and T-shirts when they exercise, hoping that no one will notice them. Invest in a few nice pieces and supportive shoes. You are much more likely to want to take that kickboxing class if you feel good about the way you are presenting yourself. Also, wearing chic exercise clothes sends the message to your subconscious that you are already fit. Frumpy, oversized clothes send the message you are not happy with your body as it currently is, so you need to hide your shape. We should accept our bodies as they are and exercise to better our health.

Chic Exercise: Mindful Morning

Tomorrow I want you to try this exercise: from the moment you wake up, make each and every movement of your morning routine slow and deliberate. As you walk to the kitchen, feel your feet in your warm and fuzzy slippers. After you pour your water and squeeze your lemon, slowly lift the glass to drink from it. Notice how the water quenches your thirst. Put the glass down with intention. When you make the kids' breakfast, breathe. Don't let them rush you. While you are slicing the mango for breakfast, notice how it smells—how the knife glides over the meat of the fruit. Chop the mango (or whatever you're preparing) with intention and love. Clear away the dishes slowly. If anything unexpected happens (your toddler spills her glass of water, the dog barks, the phone rings, you get a text message), deal with it in the present moment. Imagine you're a character in a book and don't know what's going to happen next. Be excited and curious about whatever comes your way.

You'll notice that when you slow down your movements and try to focus on what you are doing, your mind will start to wander. Big-time. You will most likely think about a "problem" that is in your life right now: something you think you might have said that offended someone, or something you did that you think displeased someone. A bill that needs to be paid and where you're going to get the money to pay for it. A pimple on your chin and how you're going to hide it for your lunch date later. Notice these thoughts entering your mind as you are trying to be aware of the present. Is it a coincidence that these thoughts are entering your mind right now? In this case, the answer is *non*.

You see, you are actually living in pleasure and clarity, and for some reason our egos like to sabotage that. So when you get a worrying thought, just observe it and let it go. I picture mine flying out of a window. You can picture yours floating away like laundry floating off the line in a windstorm. Use whatever image works for you. Then after observing and sending the thought away, go back to focusing on what you are doing. Don't hold your breath. Breathe. Get dressed slowly. Apply your makeup with purpose. Fix your hair. Notice yourself in the mirror. Notice how beautiful you are. When you are really present, your eyes will look clear and bright. Being present does wonders for one's beauty.

Another curious thing you might notice is that you start to smile. You'll catch yourself in the mirror smiling. Can it be? You are actually content! You realize that the present moment, right now, is all we have at any given moment. Right now, whatever you are doing should be focused on and celebrated. If the world were to end right now, wouldn't you rather savor each moment than be distracted and worried about the future?

We want to be chic at home, not frazzled. Without sounding too much like a hippie, we want peace and love at home. We want to be content with what we have. We want to enjoy ourselves and be a clear channel for anything and everything that comes our way. So try this exercise tomorrow morning, and you'll notice the final curious thing: this won't be just a one-time exercise; it will become a way of life.

 Out the Door

Your morning is finished and it's time to transition into afternoon. You are most likely out the door to go to work or run errands now. Are you ready for the next act of the play?

Chapter 5

THE PLEASURES
OF THE AFTERNOON

Ah, the pleasures of the afternoon. For Madame Chic, the afternoon was a welcome time to herself when the house was blissfully empty. In Paris, I was usually out every afternoon either at school or exploring the city, but the few times I stayed at home, I got to check out Madame Chic's routine. During the afternoon, she prepared lunch (usually leftovers from the previous evening, plus a small fresh salad), ran errands, and did the cleaning. Occasionally she invited girlfriends over for lunch. I remember one afternoon she asked if I wanted to join her and her friends for a light lunch of poached fish with a delicate butter sauce and haricots verts. I was impressed with Madame Chic's elegant lunch menu. No microwave dinners for her!

When you are looking after other people all day long, it can be nice to have some time to yourself in the afternoon. The older kids are at school, the little ones are napping, and you have the opportunity to get things done, uninterrupted. Take pleasure in preparing lunch, finishing a task well done, running errands, a cup of tea, and preparing for the evening meal. These very things (with the exception of tea) can often feel like chores rather than pleasures. Change your perspective to that of Madame Chic and take great pleasure in doing them. If you are only making lunch for yourself, now could be the time to experiment and try out that beet-and-goat-cheese-salad recipe you saw last week. Getting work done, even if it's returning emails and filing, can be pleasurable. Light a candle, listen to an audiobook, and roll up your sleeves. Running errands is a fantastic opportunity to get some exercise and fresh air. These tasks must be done, so we might as well derive pleasure from them.

ALBUMS FOR THE AFTERNOON

Cheek to Cheek by Vince Giordano & The Nighthawks Orchestra, Nighthawks Records, 2000.

Add some pep to your afternoon with music that will have you dancing through your day like Fred and Ginger.

Le chant des coquelicots by Amélie-les-Crayons, neômme, 2002.

This whimsical French album will make filing paperwork feel like a dream vacation in Paris (almost).

The Romeros: Celedonio, Celin, Pepe and Angel: The Royal Family of the Spanish Guitar, Decca, 1997.

Spice up your midday routine with this quintessential Spanish guitar album.

Romance of the Violin by Joshua Bell, Sony Classical, 2003.

Add romance to your afternoon with this blissful violin music . . . even if you are just peeling the potatoes.

Elis & Tom by Antônio Carlos Jobim & Elis Regina, Verve, 1974.

Relish the harmonies and glide through your day with these romantic Brazilian duets.

The Most Essential Classical Music for Your Baby (compilation), X5 Music Group, 2008.

Calm your children down after an active afternoon with this soothing and extensive compilation of classical favorites.

Debussy for Daydreaming, Philips, 1995.

If it's all feeling a bit much for you in the afternoon, take a daydreaming break with Debussy and allow your cares to fly away (even if only for a few minutes).

Tchaikovsky at Tea Time, Philips, 1996.

Make your tea party a sophisticated affair with this enchanting compilation of music.

In a Time Lapse by Ludovico Einaudi, Ponderosa Music & Art, 2013.

Many of the songs on this atmospheric classical album are inspired by great works of literature, and just might serve as muse to spark your creativity in the afternoon.

Working from Home

Working from home has its upsides and downsides. On the upside, you don't have a commute, you can set your own hours, and you can dictate your own dress code (and hopefully this dress code is chic!). On the downside, you can get cabin fever, you might feel isolated, and your work may be interrupted, especially if you have young children at home. If you work from home, try to focus on the positive aspects of your work life and go from there. Take the afternoon to really relish doing your work. Infuse love into what you do, no matter what it is. Take that positive home energy you've been cultivating and let it lift and motivate you through your working day.

Try not to get into the trap of wearing your pajamas all day (or exercise clothes), even if you don't plan on seeing anyone. Dress up for yourself, from your chic ponytail to your pretty lingerie. Dressing nicely for the day will actually keep your energy high and subconsciously motivate you to do your best work. Aim to keep your office desk as clear as possible, and try to file away your papers regularly so you don't feel discouraged by looking at tall stacks of paperwork.

Make Your Office Chic

If you work away from home, make your office or cubicle chic and cozy to inspire creativity and get you through the working day in style. Here are some ideas:

- Forgo the typical generic storage containers found in most offices. You can use mini antique orchid pots to hold your pencils and pens. Use apothecary containers to house your paper clips and rubber bands.

- Display pictures of loved ones in pretty antique frames.

- Lay out a throw rug.

- Hang art on the wall that makes you happy when you look at it.

- Place a postcard from a faraway place by your computer to conjure up great memories.

- Use potpourri or dried lavender to keep the room smelling fresh.

- Keep a luxurious shawl on the back of your chair to stay warm in the air-conditioning.

- Keep a china teacup and saucer or your favorite mug on hand for coffee and tea breaks. Bring real silverware from home to keep lunchtime dignified (even if lunch is eaten at your desk).

- Bring a bouquet of flowers from your garden or from the farmers' market and change out the water every day in the vase. It should last you all week. Or bring an orchid or African violet in to beautify your space.

✑ Lunch ✑

Lunch, even if eaten by yourself at your desk or sitting with your baby who doesn't say much, is not a throwaway meal. It is never to be scarfed down in front of your computer as you surf the Internet. It should be savored, enjoyed, and taken seriously, just like the other meals of the day.

Lunch has a different energy. I love lunch. While breakfast feels nourishing and like the opening act of the play, lunch feels like intermission. It should be fun—a welcome respite. You should eat what you want. Listen to your body. If you aren't very hungry, there is nothing wrong with having a small cup of asparagus soup and an iced tea. If you are very hungry (and likely you will be unless, of course, you just finished elevenses) why not indulge in heavier fare? If you are eating at home, try to make your presentation pretty. Even if you are eating takeout, put it on a nice plate. Aim for cloth napkins. Clear the table.

I discovered something very curious about my lunch habit while at home. I would care how the table was cleared and set for breakfast and dinner, but not lunch. I could eat lunch anywhere—my messy desk, the edge of the kitchen table piled with things. Hmm. Why didn't it matter where I took my lunch? I would never eat dinner at my desk while surfing Instagram, so why did I think it was okay to do it for lunch?

Listen, I get it. The morning can be difficult. You can be completely exhausted, and if you get five minutes to yourself for lunch, you just want to plonk in front of your laptop and peruse the gossip sites as you hurriedly eat to get some food in you. For a stay-at-home mom, lunch can feel like your only mini vacation in an otherwise relentless day of work. But while you may feel you're taking a break by zoning out as you eat, you are not doing yourself any favors, and at the end of lunch you probably won't feel so great. Why? Because you ate really fast; you didn't particularly enjoy your meal because you weren't paying attention to it; you didn't notice when you were full; you internalized all of the dramas and news on the Internet while ingesting food. Did you feel nourished at the end of it? Most likely not.

Want a real mini vacation? Even if you only have five minutes to yourself, sit down at a clear table with good posture, silverware, a plate, and a cloth napkin and slowly enjoy your lunch. We are so rushed and wired the entire day—constantly checking our iPhones, reading the news, texting our friends, checking our Facebook status, and multitasking in our heads, that it is divine bliss to tune all of that out, even for a few minutes, and focus on replenishing our energy, nourishing our bodies, and feeding our souls. You could listen to music while you do this, if you want, but sometimes silence is the most coveted thing.

If you cannot sit at a clear table and must take lunch at your desk, turn your iPhone facedown, put your computer on sleep mode, and clear a small space for yourself. Just focus on eating your food. Eat slowly. Notice how you feel. Check in with yourself. If any problems from the day threaten to rush into your head, just send them right out. There are no problems right now. You are eating lunch. If your phone buzzes, just ignore it. If you have an impulse to go online, notice the impulse and its intensity. Don't give in. Finish your lunch completely. Take a sip of your beverage. Use your napkin. Sit for a few seconds and center yourself. Give yourself that moment. Then you can go back into the fray. Check to see who texted you. Check the latest celebrity scandal online. Send that email that's been gnawing at the back of your mind. You are back into it, but at least for those blissful few moments, you were completely out of it, in your own magical world. The world of *now*.

Initially this might feel uncomfortable. But I implore you, of all the concepts in this book, take this one very seriously. Have your lunch with no distractions. No TV, no cell phone, no computer. The only exception is music. Even if you haven't had a chance to check your email all day. Even if there's an article online that you've been dying to read. Don't do it while eating lunch. Try not to think about any problems. Having lunch this way will charge your battery. It will awaken you. Otherwise you will continue to dwell in the rat race of the mind. Eating lunch this way is positively decadent and very chic.

Chic Tip

. . . .

In the evening, when you are clearing away dinner, rather than storing leftovers in large containers, make individual plates you can heat up the next day for lunch. This will save you time in the lunch hour, and it can be lovely to open the refrigerator and have a beautifully plated, well-thought-out meal waiting for you.

CANDLES FOR THE AFTERNOON

It's particularly nice in the afternoon to smell warm, comforting aromas. These fragrances embody coziness and remind us of what a luxury it is to be home during the afternoon.

vanilla

incense

sweet almond

fig

cinnamon

honey nectar

⌒ Still Moments ⌒

When you become accustomed to having a lunch with no distractions, you will start to crave this mental solitude throughout the rest of your day. Whenever you can, take a still moment. You don't have to sit down for a half-hour meditation (although that would be nice), but even two minutes of solace as you close your eyes and breathe deeply can calm you down. Unplug from the screens, the stress, and the dramas. Break up the pattern of rushing and anxiety that might be permeating your day. This pause puts things in perspective.

⌒ After-School Schedules ⌒

If you have kids, their schedules will probably dominate your afternoon. Mine are young right now, so I plan around naptime, pickups from preschool, enrichment activities, and play-dates. One thing I know for sure is I don't want to overload my children with extracurricular activities. It can be very easy to get caught up in keeping up with the Joneses who are creating little prodigies. There are children's classes for absolutely everything now. Your children could be occupied every afternoon for the rest of their lives if you so wished. But why are we so keen to sign our children up for so many after-school activities? Is it because we didn't do these activities as kids and want to make up for it? Is it because we want them to get into the best college and be as well-rounded as possible? I totally understand that, but could it also be because we are afraid of what an unscheduled afternoon looks like? Are we afraid of our children being bored?

When I was growing up, I took piano lessons once a week. On the days when I didn't have my lesson, I came home and had the entire afternoon to myself. I would play outside with the neighborhood kids until it was time for dinner (remember those days?). We would ride our bikes, climb fences and trees, create "roller coasters" in our backyard, make tents. We used our imaginations and got a lot of fresh air. On days I didn't see my friends, I was usually happy playing alone. I created a detective agency in the downstairs closet and wrote up what I thought were professional brochures and client files. I would offer to find lost cats and missing trinkets—for a small fee, naturally. And I did an awful lot of reading. I'd spend hours in our backyard with my dog, Goldie, lying on a picnic blanket in the grass reading books. Life was really good. Looking back at my childhood, I want that carefree downtime for my daughters. I don't want to be rushing them every day from school to some other activity or class. For there are many lessons to be learned from having the afternoon off.

We are overscheduling our kids, and while they might grow to have multiple skills, they are not acquiring the skill of appreciating stillness and valuing contemplation. They are not being afforded the space to dream and figure out who they want to be—what their interests are. While we no longer live in the kind of world where our children can just run around the neighborhood unsupervised until dinnertime, what would happen if we let them take over their afternoons? What would that look like? It might look like making a tent in their bedroom with sheets, brooms, and flashlights. Or it might look like creating a mud pie out of sticks, stones, mud, and worms in the backyard. They would use their imaginations, think for themselves, and create without having an adult spin on things. They would rest and unwind without being pushed by an academic or competitive agenda. They will flourish and hopefully rarely feel bored.

Right now my daughters have one to two enrichment activities a week in addition to school. Every family is different, but that feels right for us. We might schedule a playdate once a week, and we might not. We have a lot of afternoons off. I say no to a lot of invitations. Life is so full of pressure: to compete, to get in, to be seen, to be invited. It can feel like a perpetual race. As our children grow, we will constantly assess their interests and make sure they get exposure to the arts or sports that interest them. But they won't be scheduled to do something every day. They will have downtime.

Les Bébés

Everyday life can feel particularly overwhelming if you have babies or very small children. Just the trip to the car can feel epic. Recently, when I arrived at a playdate with some friends, I joked that I felt like Odysseus at the end of his journey. My rule with small children is that I do one "big" thing a day. That big thing could be a playdate at the park. Or that big thing could be going to the grocery store. With a toddler and a preschooler, one big thing is all I can personally handle.

I don't feel guilty about this because, for small children, going to the grocery store, sitting in the cart, learning about the food, and seeing all of the people can be just as exciting as going to the park. They already know how to find pleasure in everyday activities and embrace them as something that can bring joy. But if I'm tired and frazzled, then they'll think Mommy hates going to the grocery store, and what could be fun becomes an ordeal.

A friend once joked that not only do I never leave Santa Monica, I rarely let people visit Santa

Monica. If you feel overwhelmed, don't be afraid of saying no, even to your friends. If they are true friends, they will understand. You don't need to give an excuse or tell a white lie. Simply tell them the truth. "I'm feeling overwhelmed." Or even a simple "no" works just fine. Raising young children, taking care of babies, requires a lot of love, attention, and energy. You do not need to please people or try to keep up with anyone else's pace. Go at your pace. Analyze the flow of the day and make sure you are in it. If it feels slow, go slow. If you feel up for a trek across town to visit the natural history museum, go for it. Wouldn't we want our children to do the same thing—to listen to their bodies when they need to slow down?

Chic Tips

- *Enjoy the traditionally mundane parts of your day, and your children will too.*

- *If you are feeling overwhelmed and need to get things done, rethink what constitutes an activity. You don't need to always do something exciting. Going to the store to pick up milk and peaches can be your playdate for the day. Take your time and enjoy the process.*

- *Allow your children several afternoons off where they get to be in charge of their own schedules. Give them the time to relax and figure out who they want to be.*

- *Lead by example. If you want to see a change in them, look how you can implement the change in yourself.*

⌁ Beating the Energy Slumps ⌁

Even if you manage to change your perspective and learn to love your afternoon tasks, the afternoon can also bring energy slumps: bouts of boredom and dis-ease that comes from wanting to be anywhere but where we are.

In order to get maximum pleasure from the afternoon, it is important to stay current with the flow of the day. While the morning was bustling and bubbling, the afternoon may feel like more of a long stretch. Staying in the flow will require endurance.

Endurance requires embracing reality and finding inner peace with it. If you find yourself feeling bored, ask yourself why. Can you remain present and finish the task you're currently working on without labeling yourself as feeling bored? Just because you might not be doing something that is traditionally exciting does not mean that, by default, you must be bored.

If you have an energy slump, what can you do to shake it? Are you having an energy slump because that's just what people have in the afternoon? Make sure you are not plugging into a collective consciousness of what we think is typical. Sometimes when I feel like I'm having an energy slump, I challenge myself and set the timer to get a task done. I'll set it for fifteen minutes and allow myself to tidy up the living room or pay the bills (or whatever it is that needs to get done).

After a long day with the kids, I sometimes feel as though I could not possibly go on. I'm done. Toast. I check the clock and it's only three p.m. Embracing reality would be to realize that bedtime isn't for four hours, and in the meantime I have to cook dinner, clean up, give baths, and read stories. It has to get done. There is no getting around it. So is there some small flame of energy and passion that I can pull from the innermost recesses of my being to help me get through this day? Or will I give in and mope around with a bad attitude until it's all over?

The solution is to find inner peace with the situation. Yes, I'm tired. Yes, I'm looking forward to having a glass of wine and watching *House of Cards* with my husband after the kids go to bed. But can I have inner peace in my current activity, which happens to be scraping Play-Doh off the floor? The destination in my mind is relaxing after a long day. But while I'm in the midst of that long day, can I enjoy the journey to getting there? This might mean that I go a little slower when getting things done, or maybe all I need is a mental pep talk and I can shake the slump. I've surprised myself so many times by getting a second wind just when I least thought it possible.

When you banish all of the negative connotations from your afternoon, you are suddenly open to receiving all the pleasures that afternoon has to offer. You can get pleasure from anything you do in the afternoon—even if it's returning work emails and changing diapers. You are in the flow of the day.

Sometimes all it takes is an unexpected action or an inspired decision to help you get through your afternoon work. Here are some ideas, but by all means, come up with your own.

- Sniffing your wrist to smell the perfume you applied this morning.

- Listening to your current favorite album while you clean the house.

- Collapsing in your favorite armchair while you savor your afternoon cup of tea.

- Going outside for a break, taking a deep breath, and letting the sunshine hit your face or the rain touch your hair. Take your shoes off. Go barefoot in the grass. That's not something you do very often.

- Smile unexpectedly. Remember the parking structure where I walked up seven flights to get to my car? Well, as I drove a few levels down, there was a really tough biker guy (head bandanna, jean vest, and all). He was mad that the elevator wasn't opening, so he kicked the door. He turned around and saw me. I gave him a genuine smile. This tough man, who generally looked like he didn't smile much throughout the day, caught my eye and smiled back—a big toothy grin. Maybe he felt foolish that someone witnessed him kicking the elevator door. Maybe he saw my smile and it felt infectious. We shared a moment, this biker dude and I. Smile throughout your day. It will touch people in unexpected ways.

Chic Tip: Aromatic Simmer Pot

Plan on being home all afternoon? Fragrance your home the natural way with an aromatic simmer pot. Bring a small pot of water to boil on the stove. Add the peel and rinds of your favorite fruits along with spices and/or oils and allow the mixture to boil for a few minutes. Then turn the heat to low and let the aromatic mixture simmer for as long as you'd like—just be sure to add water every thirty minutes so the ingredients don't burn. Add the peels from lemons, oranges, apples, or pineapple, a few cinnamon sticks and cloves in the winter, or a few drops of vanilla in the warmer months. Your home will smell heavenly. Just don't forget to turn off the stove before leaving the house.

Declutter Project du Jour

I find it helpful to pick one declutter project of the day. I usually do this in the afternoon, but you can do it whenever it suits your schedule. This can be as simple as checking your hot spots and clearing them. Or it could be clearing out one pantry shelf or one bathroom drawer. Take a moment to add love back to your home.

Here are some ideas for a declutter project du jour:

- Dump out the contents of your purse and edit them. Clean and organize your purse on a regular basis.

- Sort through the contents of the container where you keep your incoming items (keys, mail, etc.) and organize.

- Tackle a drawer: organize the contents of your nightstand drawer, the kitchen junk drawer, the desk drawer.

- Clear out your underwear drawer and throw away any old undergarments. Arrange your bras and panties in a beautiful and organized fashion. You'll smile tomorrow when you reach in to get your undergarments.

- Take the basket on the stairs upstairs and put things back in their proper spaces.

- Don't forget your car! Clean out trash, junk, and other items that don't belong there.

- Enlist help! You don't need to do any of this by yourself (except maybe for your purse and your underwear drawer).

Vinegar Multipurpose Cleaner

1 cup water

1 cup distilled (white) vinegar

40 drops of lavender oil or tea tree oil

Mix all ingredients in a glass spray bottle and store in a cool, dark place.

....

The lavender really does cut through the vinegar smell. I have grown completely addicted to this scent. To me it smells "clean." The lavender and vinegar both have antibacterial properties. The vinegar is a multipurpose cleaner in itself that is nontoxic, good for the environment, and actually holds up well in comparison to most commercial cleaners. This is my favorite cleaner and I always have a batch on hand. In fact, I love it so much that over the holidays I'll make batches for my neighbors and friends, with the recipe attached to the glass spray bottle by a big bow. Hey, when they're cleaning, maybe they'll think of me!

⟶ Menu Planning ⟵

If you want to make your life easier, sit down with your cookbooks and plan out the menu for the coming week. Write up your grocery list so you aren't wandering aimlessly at the grocery store buying things you don't need. (I cannot tell you how many times I've done this.) Post the week's menu on the refrigerator so that everyone knows what to look forward to. Don't be afraid to embrace a regular schedule. Perhaps every Monday in winter you cook a fabulous vegetable stew and serve it with warm loaves of crusty bread with butter. Tuesday might be taco night. Switch up the ingredients you use to keep your palate interested. Serve fish tacos or veggie tacos one week instead of the usual chicken, for example.

While I never noticed Madame Chic sitting down to

write out the week's menu, we always had a hot, three-course (minimum!) meal on the table every evening. This regular feat could not be pulled off without planning, so whether she sat down to write a list before grocery shopping or kept a mental list in her head (this probably comes naturally after doing it for so many years), her meals were a hit every time and something we all looked forward to.

Emulate Madame Chic by becoming a connoisseur of a handful of dishes. Perfect them. Explore their nuances. Having routines and traditions does not have to be boring. For taco Tuesdays, become a connoisseur of tacos. In the summertime I make my own fresh heirloom tomato salsa. We normally have chicken tacos, and I've found just the perfect spice rub for the meat. We try to always include fresh avocados and cilantro from our herb pot outside the front door. In the winter I use our favorite jarred salsas—smoky peach salsa for that sweet kick, or habanero lime salsa for spicy and tangy cravings. We have fun trying different cheeses. My husband tries to avoid wheat, so he has corn tortillas. We have turned taco Tuesdays into an art. They are never boring.

Keep the seasons in mind when planning your menu. You probably won't want to cook your famous shepherd's pie in the middle of summer. Create two catalogs of your favorite recipes: one for warm weather and one for cold. Enjoy fresh vegetables, barbecue, and watermelon in the summer and hearty stews and savory pies in the winter.

Chic Afternoon Pastimes

Take some time each afternoon to do something beautiful. It is wonderful to take a break from the work of the afternoon and focus on something that brings you joy.

- Write a letter to a faraway friend . . . and mail it.

- Arrange some beautiful bouquets of flowers (place one bouquet in your children's rooms to give them a pleasant surprise).

- Work on your family scrapbook or picture album.

- Sit down in your reading nook and cuddle up with a great book.

- Go out on your balcony and do some stretching.

- Write in your poetry journal; work on your poems for a few minutes every day.

- Play the piano for twenty minutes (I do this almost every day. It *feeds* my soul).

- Tend to your orchids and other houseplants by watering or pruning them. Don't forget to dust their leaves.

- Don your sun hat and gardening gloves and spend a half hour in your garden tending to your plants.

- Take on a new hobby and devote some time to it every afternoon. Practice calligraphy, learn a new language, compose some music, edit your family films, make homemade jam, knit, needlepoint . . . whatever you fancy.

⁓ Preparing Dinner ⁓

One of the pleasures of the afternoon is thinking about dinner. You will already have planned your weekly menu and have the ingredients on hand. Now comes the prep work. If you are making a shepherd's pie, perhaps now you could boil and mash the potatoes. Whatever you can do to make this evening's meal prep less hectic is welcome here. Cook the rice for the curry, prep the vegetables, do whatever you can do. If you are not at home during the afternoon, consider prepping food in the morning in the slow cooker, for example, or even the night before. You can peel and chop the vegetables beforehand and store them in the fridge. If you take care of all the time-consuming things first, it will be easier to finish the dish when the dinner crunch time arrives. This also cuts down on the mess.

⁓ Meal Prep Mondays ⁓

Pick one day a week when you prep for several meals in the upcoming week. It's Monday afternoon and you're starting to prepare the dinner for tonight. While you have everything out and are going to get the kitchen messy, you might as well accomplish a lot more than making just one meal. During this time I get out a few cutting boards, the rice cooker, and the storage containers. I preheat the oven. I'll roast vegetables and cook enough brown rice for a few meals and cook some lentils on the stove. If I don't want to roast the carrots right now, for example, I'll peel them, slice them up, and put them in a ziplock bag so that they are ready for roasting a few nights later.

This is what I did this Monday: I peeled and sliced two bunches of carrots. I roasted five sweet potatoes and a whole head of garlic. I baked four jacket potatoes and four red bell peppers. I simmered a pot of lentils on the stove. I made two cups' worth of brown rice in the rice cooker. I chopped and sautéed tofu with a sweet soy glaze. (We eat several vegetarian meals during the week.) I made peas on the stove. For dinner that night we had baked potatoes and peas with lamb chops that my husband prepared. For the rest of the week I have the rice prepared, the red peppers roasted (I put them in a ziplock bag as soon as I take them out of the oven, then drizzle them with olive oil and a pinch of salt. The skin comes off nicely this way, and they are so delicious to eat cold the next day). Each week it's a little different. But preparing all of these items in advance makes my week so much easier. Then as the week goes on, I only have one or two things to prepare each night for dinner rather than having to concoct an entire meal.

You can precook certain meats, precook pasta, or make a large pot of soup and freeze half. I choose Monday to prep meals because I have the entire week ahead of me and I'm usually feeling energetic. By Thursday, when I'm running low on steam, it's nice to not have to worry about giving my kids a healthy meal. It's all prepared and within reach.

Chic Tip

. . . .

Whenever the family and I go on an all-day outing, I like to prepare a meal in the slow cooker in the morning before we leave. Slow-cooker meals usually take no time to prepare at all, yet they cook all day long, filling the house with their mouthwatering aroma. By the time you get home, they are hot and ready to eat.

Our most recent outing was at the La Brea Tar Pits. Trekking across town to look at all of those dinosaur fossils sure built up our appetites. We had lunch while we were there, but when we got home in the late afternoon, I was able to decompress after the trip because our pot roast was already prepared. Serving dinner that night was easy and put a nice cap on the end of our day.

Signature Dish

When I was a kid, we would drive a few times every summer to visit our parents' friends Tom and Nancy. They had a pool, which, for my sister and me, was just the coolest thing ever. Every time we visited, Tom would light up the barbecue and make his famous tri-tip steak. He always served it with salad and baked potatoes. The marinade for his steak was so flavorful—the meat itself so tender. Eating Tom's steak dinner was something I looked forward to almost as much as swimming in their pool. To this day, it was the nicest tri-tip I've ever had. Food can trigger very powerful memories in us, and the people you love will remember you by your beautiful dish.

Madame Chic was a traditionalist in everything, from the way she decorated her apartment to the way she prepared her ratatouille, so naturally her signature dishes were all French classics. Most nights we would have a protein of some sort, mainly chicken, fish, or an omelet. The meat was always served with a classic French sauce such as *beurre blanc* or velouté. Sautéed vegetables or her famous ratatouille would serve as a side dish. As is traditional in France, these main courses would be followed by a salad. Madame Chic's signature desserts included her marvelous apple tart, crème caramel, and orange liqueur fruit salad, which were all prepared on a regular basis.

Fancy Parisian Fruit Salad

Madame Chic made this fruit salad for both her family and special guests. Served in a footed crystal bowl, this re-freshing dessert makes a spectacular grand finale. Here is my take on her recipe.

6–8 cups chopped fresh fruit (any combination of the following: strawberries, bananas, grapes, kiwi, mango, oranges, raspberries, blueberries, pear, apple)

¼–½ cup Grand Marnier (depending on how strong you'd like the orange liqueur flavor and how much fruit you use)

¼ cup orange juice

1–2 tablespoons granulated sugar

Chopped mint for garnish

Peel and chop your fruit, keeping all pieces at a consistent size. Place fruit in a decorative bowl. Pour Grand Marnier and orange juice on top of the fruit. Sprinkle the sugar over the mixture. Mix well. Scatter chopped mint lightly over the top. Serve on pretty plates.

. . . .

Chic Tip: Signature Recipe Cookbook

. . . .

Combine all of your favorite recipes in a small binder and keep this as your signature recipe cookbook. Cut out recipes from magazines, print from the Internet, or photocopy them from your favorite cookbooks. This way you will have all of your favorites in one handy place. Whenever you are menu planning and feel at a loss for what to prepare, you will be inspired when you open this homemade book full of your family's favorite recipes. Some of the signature dishes included in my repertoire are: shepherd's pie, leek and cheese pie, spinach and goat cheese tart, honey soy chicken, chicken tacos, maple-glazed salmon, leek and potato soup, lentils and rice, beef stew with dumplings, slow-cooker pot roast with potatoes and carrots, apple pie, berry crumble, and flourless chocolate cake.

⟋⟋⟋ Outings ⟋⟋⟋

We don't get to have them every day, but afternoon outings are an important part of maintaining balance in our life. We all work so hard, we deserve to have fun and do something out of the ordinary, even if we are alone (actually, it can be quite pleasurable if we are alone). Go have tea in the local museum garden or get some popcorn and catch an afternoon film. Just do something for the sake of pleasure. Go by yourself if no one will go with you. It is important to carve out this time for ourselves.

If you've been working too hard, you need to take a break. Ideally you will take many breaks. Even if it's just for an hour. While the kids are in school, can you sit at the bluffs and watch the sea? When your spouse gets home at night, can you go get dinner with your girlfriends every now and then? My friend Lisa told me her neighbor, who has young twin boys, often leaves the house after her husband gets home and goes to eat sushi by herself. It is her own mini vacation. Outings can be as simple as watching the ducks in your local park or as involved as taking an art tour at your favorite museum. Outings help us decompress and relish the afternoon.

⌒◦ Mail ◦⌒

Delight in the daily routine of dealing with the mail. When it arrives, go through it immediately and recycle any opened envelopes or junk mail. Put the bills in the same place each time so that you can pay them on time, and then file them away. It's best to reserve one drawer for supplies of stamps, pens, envelopes, and whatever other things you need. I swear, for the past ten years of my life I was always muttering, "Where are all the pens?" and "Where did I put the stamps?" To be fair, my daughters think the stamps are actually stickers, so I tend to hide them in different places. If you have young children and this is the case, just keep the stamps in the same out-of-reach spot until your children are older and won't decorate their Hello Kitty lunch boxes with your brand-new book of Forever Stamps.

This month develop a routine for collecting, sorting, paying, and filing away your bills. Don't deviate from your routine. You'll find after one month of consistent action that you will have developed a habit that will now come to you as second nature. Not only will your new mail routine make you efficient and organized, but you will never forget to pay a bill again.

~ Paying Your Bills ~

Speaking of paying bills . . . once you sit down to actually pay them, pay attention to how you feel. Do you have a steady stream of panic flowing through your system? Are you thinking negative thoughts about money? Are you racked with worry and anxiety? I used to be. If I received a large bill of any kind (heck, even a small bill), I would be riddled with anxiety. This subtle but substantial shift in energy would stay with me until the next time I opened the mail.

If this is you, try an exercise the next time you pay your bills. Be aware the instant a negative thought about money and finance enters your head. Notice what your thoughts are saying: *"If I pay this, I won't be able to go out next week." "Why am I always broke?" "I never have any money." "Why can't I just get ahead?" "Whenever I get any money, I always get a bill and it just goes away."* Just be the witness to these negative thoughts. Then notice how they make you feel. I bet even reading them gave you the heebie-jeebies. (I got the heebie-jeebies from just writing them!) Take that anxiety you feel and allow it to pass through you. Don't let it get stuck on the way. Acknowledge the feeling, but don't hold on to it. Release it. Once you are able to banish these thoughts and empower yourself, you can become a clear channel able to attract more prosperity. It may sound kooky, but I'm completely serious.

If it is helpful, consciously replace those thoughts with positive affirmations about money. *I have plenty of money to pay this bill. I am prosperous. I am responsible with money. Everything is going to be okay.* To this very day, whenever I pay a bill, I sit tall with good posture and mindfully write out the check. I make it a point to be very present. In the beginning I would banish negative thoughts about money immediately by noticing them, letting them burn through me, and then sending them away. Now I don't get the negative thoughts anymore. I pay every bill on time. This is not magic; this is just consciousness. This does not mean that I can run up my credit card bill by going on shopping sprees and talk myself out of feeling anxiety; I'm still responsible with money. This consciousness makes me even more responsible with money because it gives me clarity. Often we act out our anxiety by shopping even more. We figure that we are broke, so we might as well go for broke on a spending spree. No, this clarity with paying the bills gives you clarity with spending money too. You will be able to weed through the lower energies and only buy quality items that you need.

⁓ Afternoon Tea ⁓

"Better to be deprived of food for three
days than tea for one."

—Ancient Chinese Proverb

TEA GUIDE

Black Tea: strong, full-bodied, caffeinated teas generally hailing from Sri Lanka, India, and China.

English Breakfast: a strong blend of various black teas (usually Assam) intended to be taken with milk (sugar optional) at breakfast.

Earl Grey: aromatic black tea with bergamot and citrus oil. The strong flavor is nicely offset by milk and sugar. This is a popular tea for the afternoon.

Chai: a spiced blend of black tea, ginger, cardamom, cinnamon, fennel, clove, and black pepper. Served with milk and sugar, it is suitable for both morning and afternoon consumption.

Darjeeling: a delicate floral tea that is best served alone or with a slice of lemon. Delightful in the afternoon.

Assam: A full-bodied Indian black tea with a rich,

tarry flavor. Can be taken with milk and sugar. A popular tea for morning and afternoon.

Ceylon: a bold black tea from Sri Lanka with citrus notes. This tea can be served with milk, sugar, and/or lemon and is lovely in the afternoon.

Lapsang Souchong: a bold, smoky black tea. This one is not for the faint of heart. Most people either love it or hate it. Will appeal to those who enjoy bitter-sweet, roasted flavors. Can be taken with lemon and sugar.

Oolong Tea: a mildly caffeinated traditional Chinese tea whose taste ranks between black tea and green tea. Oolong tea has been linked to weight loss. It has a delightful, delicate flavor that can stand alone without the addition of milk or sugar. Fine for morning or afternoon consumption.

Green Tea: a caffeinated tea that originates in China and Japan. Packed with antioxidants, green tea is known for its immense health benefits. All green teas are delicious alone but can also be served with honey or lemon. Suitable for morning and afternoon consumption.

Gunpowder: the most popular variety of Chinese green tea, in which the leaves are rolled into tight pellets that open up during the brewing process.

Dragonwell: has a smooth, toasty flavor.

Sencha: a light, refreshing Japanese green tea in which the leaves look like tiny needles.

Jasmine: Jasmine tea is a blend of green teas that is infused with the essence of jasmine blossoms. Jasmine tea carries a sensational aroma and is lovely for a sensory tea.

White Tea: a lightly caffeinated tea known for its high antioxidant count. Many white teas are blended with fruit or floral notes (peach white tea is lovely). Light in color, white teas have a delicate, subtle, and mild taste and pair well with honey.

Herbal Tea: a blend of herbs, spices, and other plant material, herbal teas contain no caffeine and have a plethora of health benefits due to their high antioxidant count. There are too many varieties of herbal teas to list in this chapter, so I am mentioning the most popular here. Because they are caffeine free, they can be consumed any time of day and late into the evening without disrupting sleep. Many of the digestive teas are wonderful to have after a large meal.

Chamomile: famous for aiding upset stomachs and promoting sleep, chamomile is a mild herbal tea with a pale yellow color once brewed. It is best taken alone or with lemon and honey.

Ginseng: made from the ginseng root, this tea is a popular digestive aid and is wonderful to drink when you are feeling under the weather. With its strong, pungent taste, ginseng tea is lovely when paired with lemon and honey.

Lemon and Ginger: remember my cheeky signature drink of hot water with lemon? Lemon tea is so easy to make. Take hot water and squeeze half a lemon into the cup. Add honey and grated ginger, if desired. This is another great drink for when you are feeling under the weather.

Peppermint: steep peppermint leaves in hot water to get not only a delicious tea but also a digestive aid, stress reliever, and weight-loss promoter all in one cup. Lovely served with honey.

Rosehip: rosehips are the part of the rose just below the petals. They are fabulous for treating colds and flu and for aiding digestion (noticing a trend here?). With a mild, floral taste, rosehip tea has a beautiful deep-pink color and is very aromatic.

Rooibos: also known as red-bush tea, rooibos comes from Africa and has a mild, smooth taste and a deep ruby-red color. Rooibos tea can be drunk by itself or paired with milk and sugar.

Ah, that delightful time of day for afternoon tea. Whether you celebrate by having a quiet cup while reading a book, or you invite a few friends over for tea, sandwiches, and scones, afternoon tea is a great way to honor the afternoon. It's another low-stress way to entertain, much like brunch and elevenses. You can make your afternoon teas as simple or elaborate as you'd like.

Here are three variations of afternoon tea you can choose, depending on the formality of your celebration.

Casual Affair

This is really simple. Invite one or two friends over, put the kettle on, and have some cookies laid out on a fancy plate, or provide a simple cake. Often when I make cakes, I double the batch and put one in the freezer to save for later. Or if I'm making loaf cake, like a pound or almond cake, I'll bake it in small loaf pans. So many times we will make a large cake and only eat a portion of it, allowing the rest to go bad over the next few days. If you make smaller cakes, use one and freeze the others; this way you will never waste the delicious cake. This is the type of afternoon tea I have most often. And I find it's the most intimate.

This summer I had two girlfriends who both had new babies over for tea. I made a blueberry cake. They were exhausted from lack of sleep. So they were really happy to see a homemade cake and the pot of tea waiting for them. It was so nice to sit and laugh and connect this way.

Blueberry Cake

½ cup butter, room temperature

½ cup sugar

1 teaspoon vanilla extract

¼ teaspoon salt

2 egg yolks

1½ cups all-purpose flour

1 teaspoon baking powder

⅓ cup milk

1½ cups fresh blueberries

2 egg whites

¼ cup sugar

1 tablespoon all-purpose flour

1 tablespoon sugar

Preheat oven to 350 degrees F. Grease and flour an 8-inch baking pan. Cream the butter and ½ cup of sugar. Add vanilla and salt. Separate the eggs and reserve the whites. Add yolks to the sugar mixture and beat until creamy. Combine 1½ cups of flour and baking powder and add it alternately with the milk to the egg-yolk mixture. Coat the berries with 1 tablespoon of flour (this prevents them from sinking to the bottom of the cake) and add them to the batter. Mix with a spoon to avoid breaking up the berries. In a different bowl, beat the egg whites until soft peaks form. Gradually add ¼ cup of sugar and keep beating until stiff peaks form. Fold the egg whites into the main batter. Pour into your prepared pan. Sprinkle the top with the last tablespoon of sugar. Bake for 50 minutes or until the cake is set.

. . . .

◦ A Slightly More Formal Affair ◦

You can add a few sandwiches to the casual tea mentioned above for a more substantial tea. Here are some of my favorites:

Cream cheese cucumber

Spread cream cheese on one side of the bread. Peel alternate strips of cucumber, leaving about half of the dark peel on. Slice the cucumber thinly and layer on the bread. Trim the crusts off and cut into dainty triangles.

One-step deli salad sandwiches

If I don't have a lot of time to prepare sandwiches, I'll buy a small container of curry chicken or cranberry tuna salad from our local deli. All you need to do is scoop these prepared salads onto fresh bread, cut the crusts off, and cut into triangles. Add fresh greens like lettuce or an herb such as dill to give it that almost-homemade touch.

Egg salad sandwich

Boil four or five eggs (or more, depending on how many people you'll be serving). Once the egg is hard-boiled, remove the shell and mash with a fork. Place a few spoonfuls of mayonnaise (I actually prefer to use Veganaise) until you are happy with the consistency. Mash together. Sprinkle paprika and add salt and pepper to your taste. Mix it all together. Add a small spoonful of sweet relish, if desired. Place between two slices of fresh bread, cut off the crusts, and cut into triangles.

Watercress sandwich

My Victorian American Girl doll, Samantha, loved eating watercress sandwiches for tea (I know this from the books, you see), so I naturally loved them too. Take fresh white or wheat bread, spread your favorite herbed cheese on one slice, and place clean watercress on top. Cut off crusts and cut into triangles. Serve.

Vegan tea sandwich

For delicious vegan tea sandwiches, you have many options. Try hummus and sliced cucumber with salt and pepper. Try Veganaise and avocado. Use a vegan cream cheese and combine it with mixed chopped herbs. You can also use any shredded vegetable you enjoy, such as carrots or radishes. Get creative. Enjoy!

⤳ A Formal Affair ᴄ

For a formal affair, use any of the above, but also add a few treats like champagne (champagne and tea . . . why not?), cupcakes, and scones with clotted cream and jam. Dress the table with a beautiful cloth. Pick some flowers from the garden or buy a beautiful bouquet of flowers. Delight in the presentation.

Vanilla Cupcakes with Real Strawberry Frosting

1 cup white sugar

½ cup butter

2 eggs

2 teaspoons vanilla extract

1½ cups all-purpose flour

1¾ teaspoons baking powder

½ cup milk

Preheat your oven to 350 degrees F. Line a cupcake pan with paper liners. Cream the butter and sugar together. Beat in the eggs and then stir in the vanilla. Add the flour and baking powder and mix well. Stir in the milk until you have a smooth batter. Spoon into the lined cups. Fill the cups no more than three-quarters of the way with batter so they don't have a "muffin top." Bake 25 minutes or until a toothpick inserted into the middle of the cake comes out clean.

Real Strawberry Frosting

1 cup fresh strawberries

1 cup butter

1 cup confectioners' sugar, sifted

1 teaspoon vanilla extract

2½ cups confectioners' sugar, sifted

Puree the strawberries in a blender. Place strawberry puree in a saucepan and cook over medium heat until it is brought to a boil. Stay close and stir it often until the puree is reduced by half, which takes around 15–20 minutes. Remove the strawberry reduction from the heat and allow it to cool. Beat the butter in a mixer until light and fluffy. Then add the first cup of sifted confectioners' sugar. Add the vanilla extract. While the mixer is beating, alternate between adding the remaining 2½ cups of the sifted confectioners' sugar and spoonfuls of the strawberry reduction, until the sugar and strawberries are all incorporated. This will be the best frosting you've ever made.

. . . .

Bouquets for Tea Parties (or Anytime)

The best way to keep your bouquets fresh for as long as possible is to change the water in the vase every day. Nothing works quite like this. No need for sugar or bleach in the water. The flowers just long for fresh water.

Pink roses bouquet

Take a dozen or more pink roses of different shades (fuchsia, baby pink, double delight, peach, plum, and cream, for example) and trim the stems so they just peek out of the top of a small round vase. Once the stem is trimmed to the correct length, hold the first rose in your left hand, then add the next one and the next one so that the stems spiral around each other and look presentable once placed in the vase. The fullness of the roses just peeking out over the top of the vase is beautiful enough on its own without a filler.

Lilac and lavender bouquet

Create a beautiful and fragrant purple bouquet of lilac and cut lavender. Place a few strong lilac sprays in a medium vase and fill the empty spaces with lavender and another filler such as larkspur or million aster in lavender or cream hues.

Romantic red-and-white bouquet

In a medium-sized vase, place a dozen or more red roses. Trim the stems of the rose so that the flowers stick out one or two inches above the top of the base. Take any white fillers, such as double stock or wax flowers, and arrange them in the empty spots so that they are just slightly taller than the red roses. For an added layer of depth and aroma, place a green herb, such as lemon verbena, in select areas throughout the bouquet.

LES FLEURS

Whether you pick them from your own garden or get them from the farmers' market or the deli downtown, bringing home a bouquet of flowers does not have to be only for special occasions. Keep a bouquet in the entry-way or on the dining table that everyone can enjoy. Take a few flowers from the main bouquet and create smaller bouquets, placing them around the house in unexpected places like your bathroom, children's room, or kitchen. Each week I snip off a few geraniums from our window box and place them in a crystal bud vase in our powder room. Those cheerful pink blooms may be small, but they brighten up the space beautifully.

You don't have to have fancy crystal vases for all of your bouquets. Mason jars, old jam jars, orchid pots (without holes), antique ginger jars, and empty candle jars all make very chic vases.

If you are running short on flowers, try pairing a few wildflowers with an herb such as basil, rosemary, or lemon verbena for a delightful fragrance combination. Or put cut lavender and rosemary or sage in a bud vase for a charming pairing.

After a really euphoric afternoon tea, it can sometimes be hard to transition back into the rest of our day. We wish we could float off on a cloud of teacups, pearls, and vanilla cupcakes with strawberry frosting. But back to the day we must get. Shall we?

A Word on Television

We all have our favorite shows. It's a good idea to be conscious about the way we watch television, however, and not just have it constantly on in the background, filling the gaps in our day with noise and frenetic energy. A recent *USA Today* study was released showing that even background television that is not being watched by children can distract them and negatively impact their attention. Plus, as adults we become numb to what's shown on TV. Inappropriate ads for health problems (you know the kind I mean), daytime talk shows where ex-couples are screaming at each other about paternity tests, and reality shows showcasing nasty catfights add an icky, hostile element to your family home. I used to be oblivious to all of this before I had kids. Now it's as if I see everything through their eyes, so now the TV is off unless we have an actual show we want to watch. No more channel surfing for us.

⟶ Getting through a Difficult Day ⟵

So what about those worst-case scenario days? How can we get through those days without feeling overwhelmed? Here's an example: your toddler, who has a history of febrile seizures, complains of not feeling well. You take her temperature and she has a 103.2-degree fever. It's the middle of the night. You call the emergency doctor and they advise you what to do. You and the family are up at three a.m. trying to make her feel better. Everyone goes back to sleep at five thirty, only to have the baby wake up at six a.m., ready to go. Your day has begun and you've had four hours of sleep.

Even though you're tired and your oldest child is not feeling well, everything still needs to get done: breakfast, lunch, snack, and dinner. Because the sick child is not going to school, the kids are in the living room all day with a bit of cabin fever. The mess has started to accumulate, but because you're so tired, you simply cannot bring yourself to pick anything up. You have to take your toddler to the doctor, but the babysitter is not only out of town but out of the country, so your husband stays home from work in the morning to watch the baby.

After the doctor's visit, you go to the pharmacy with your

toddler to get the medicine as quickly as possible. The lines are long and people are impatient. You also quickly stop at the grocery store to get some watermelon (toddler's request) and Popsicles (doctor's recommendation, which toddler happily agrees to). Finally you get home and your husband, after checking that all is okay, leaves quickly to get back to work. You have the two kids all to yourself for the next six hours, and even though your back hurts and you are physically and mentally exhausted, you have got to press on.

How am I able to write this scenario in such vivid detail? It's what happened to us last week! I know every parent can relate to this. At some point children get sick and everything needs to be put on hold. What we thought would happen (school, work, playdates) is no longer happening. I did stray to hopelessness a few times and at one point felt like crying. The load of work to be done—food preparation, general tidying up—it all seemed like too much for me to take on. I felt terrible for my daughter, who didn't feel well (although you would never have known it from the way she was chatting away with the doctor!). I felt bitter that my husband could just leave and go to work. I didn't have that ability, to just leave for a few hours and come back, refreshed.

Thankfully, I caught myself. I saw where this was all going. I was starting to let bitterness and negative thinking ruin my day. I thought about how I could turn this situation around and get back on track. First and foremost, I decided to slow down. I talk about flow a lot, and the flow of this day was very different from how I pictured it would be. The dis-ease was happening because I was fighting against the flow. A normal weekday would see us in hustle-and-bustle mode, with my daughter going to school and the baby and I running errands together and playing. Because we had all had no sleep and my oldest child was sick, the flow of the day had slowed down significantly, yet I was still trying to hustle and bustle.

First step: I slowed down. Pause. Okay, so things weren't going how I'd pictured. I needed to get over it. First priority: making sure my older daughter was comfortable and getting rest. I turned on some soothing music, put my apron on, and created a little area on a soft blanket for the girls to play on. I opened the windows to get some fresh air in. With the music and the open windows, the atmosphere in the house had already shifted. I went into the kitchen and started the preparations for the evening's meal, country fish pie (an English specialty and favorite of my husband). I decided to think of peeling the potatoes as a wonderful meditative action rather than a chore, a chance to focus on one task and enjoy this domestic moment. The girls, playing on their blanket, were actually having fun doing something out of the ordinary.

I made my fish pie. While the pie baked, I lay down on the sofa while they played. The afternoon went on. Cartoons were watched, books were read, a mess was made that eventually was cleared away (not perfectly, but perfect enough for that day). When my husband came home, we went to the dinner table and had fish pie and those doctor-prescribed Popsicles for dessert.

I looked at what I could appreciate in the day, for there was so much: my daughter's viral infection was not too serious and she was going to be fine; my baby was still in good health; the doctor had been able to see us at the last minute; we live close to the pharmacy; my husband has a job that allows him to help watch the baby while I took her sister to the doctor; I had done my meal planning and grocery shopping for the week, so I had a delicious dinner to prepare and didn't have to order takeout; we had an enjoyable day slowing down, cooking, playing, and just being in the new flow of the day.

So when something negative happens and changes the trajectory of your day and things just seem to be going wrong right and left, pause. "Things going wrong" is a sign for you to change into the new flow of the day. How can you change your circumstance and bring yourself back to joy? What can you be grateful for? To do this, you must let go of how you thought the day would go. Let it go and embrace what the day has become.

Before we conclude this story, I wanted to tell you about the pharmacy visit. Remember I said the line was long? A store clerk, who was attuned to the moment, spotted me with my sick child. He caught my eye and quietly ushered me to the front of the new line he started. I thanked him and told him I was grateful for his helping us because my daughter was ill. He said, "My pleasure, ma'am." I am grateful for that store clerk and his act of kindness. I'm grateful he was present enough in his job to be able to spot me from the line and do a good deed. I hope his kindness is returned to him tenfold.

Chic Tip: Meditation in Activity

. . . .

Zen Buddhist Hakuin Ekaku said, "Meditation in the midst of activity is a thousand times superior to meditation in stillness." He put into words everything I aspire to throughout my day. After all, it is easy to be calm and have inner peace while you are alone in your house, doing something for yourself, such as reading a book, gardening, or cooking a leisurely meal on a Sunday afternoon. But what about four p.m. on a Wednesday afternoon? You're in the middle of the kitchen with a baby tugging at your dress and a toddler jumping on the sofa like it's a trampoline. You're trying to make dinner. The dog needs to go out. You need to post the bills before the mail carrier comes. The teakettle starts to squeal. Can you achieve a state of inner peace throughout all of this? Because if you can, you have won. You are practicing meditation in activity. And that is our goal. That is chic. Being in the flow and cultivating peace no matter what happens throughout our busy, bubbling, hectic, chaotic, messy, fabulous day.

ALBUMS FOR THE COMMUTE HOME

100 Most Relaxing Classical Music in the Universe (compilation), Denon, 2010.

The title of this album pretty much says it all, but these classical favorites will soothe your mind after a long day. You'll float all the way home.

Chopin: The Complete Piano Works Waltzes by Rem Urasin, Krzysztof Jablonski, Tatyana Shebanova, IMC Music, 2010.

There's just something about the piano. When your brain feels fried, it is one of those comforting sounds that can restore you to sanity.

Relaxation: Nature's Soothing Sounds (compilation), Echo Bridge Home Entertainment, 2005.

When you've been sitting under fluorescent lights all day, sometimes you just want to be immersed in nature. So why not listen to ocean waves, thunderstorms, and other natural soundscapes on the way home?

Native American Flutes & the Sounds of Nature by Jessica Reyes, Talking Taco Music, 2010.

Wash away any worries from the workplace with the tranquil sounds of the Native American flute.

The Romantic Harp by Judy Loman, Naxos, 2005.

Quell any potential road rage by listening to this peaceful and melodious album.

Putumayo Presents: Latin Beat (compilation), Putumayo World Music, 2012.

If you're going out after work and need to pump yourself up, listening to this passionate album will give you that much-needed second wind.

Elements by Ira Stein and Russel Walder, Windham Hill Records, 1990.

If you can get ahold of this amazing album, your breath will be taken away by the rapturous piano and oboe harmonies. It is the perfect music to listen to after a long day in the office.

Chapter 6

THE PLEASURES
OF THE EVENING

Twilight is one of the most magnificent times of day. The light is different. The air is different. The perfume of flowers seems to grow stronger. The hectic day is almost over and we can rest.

For many busy parents, twilight means that the kids' bedtime is nigh and we can enjoy some downtime. For those with really small children, you can go to the bathroom uninterrupted! You can take a shower and blow-dry your hair without having someone tug at your leg! You can read your book without having a little person (albeit a very cute little person) try to take it away from you! We love our children but after an entire day tending to their needs, it's nice to have time to ourselves in the evening hours.

Sure, most nights are ordinary and you will stay at home. But how divine it can be to luxuriate in the ordinariness of a typical evening. To walk around a quiet house after everyone's gone to bed, turning out the lights and closing the curtains. Taking a long, hot bath in fragrant oils. Having a cup of tea and enjoying a good book. Watching a riveting show on television. Going to sleep at 7:30 p.m. if you're extra-exhausted and waking up completely refreshed. Even though your evening might be an ordinary one, taking pleasure in its simplicity makes it extraordinary.

It's nice to take part in a twilight ritual, even if it's only on special occasions. Whenever we would visit my grandmother Lila in Cambria, the beautiful seaside town where she lived, she would rally the entire family to go to the beach each evening to watch the sunset. She was a connoisseur of twilight. She'd tell us all to make a wish as we saw the sun sink into the ocean. I remember many memorable twilights sitting on those beautiful California bluffs. We'd be wrapped in our Windbreakers, bracing ourselves in the sharp ocean breezes and looking down on the rocky cliffs below, laughing, excited to have our family reunited together. Grandma was adamant that we make a wish as the sun set. She insisted that it was her lifelong sunset wishes that granted her her beautiful house in Cambria. It probably was the powerful combination of intention, appreciation, and presence in nature that granted her wish and drove her to get her house. Twilight unites our family whenever we get together. And whenever I'm able to watch the sunset, I do it, and think of my grandmother.

～◌ Cocktail Hour ◌～

When I lived in Paris, twilight was aperitif time. Before Madame Chic's dinner parties we'd sip our whiskeys, ports, or tomato juices while listening to classical music—the men still in their suits for the day, the women in skirts and dresses. Chez Madame Bohemienne we would gather on the sofa round a fizzing bowl of champagne cocktail, laughing and listening to jazz music. Aperitif time was not about the beverage (although they do help to whet your appetite for the meal ahead) but about the ritual of gathering, conversing, and connecting before breaking bread.

In other parts of the world, this time is called cocktail hour. While I don't take part in this indulgence every day, cocktail hour can be fun. My very favorite cocktail is the Kir Royale, a wonderful French cocktail composed of champagne and crème de cassis liqueur. It is my cocktail of choice whenever I'm out. When I have one, I am transported to Paris, sitting in one of those gilded and glittery bars sounded by chic intellects. Sigh.

Kir Royale

1 part crème de cassis

5 parts champagne

Pour crème de cassis into a champagne flute and slowly pour the champagne on top.

....

My friend Juliana throws a Werewolf cocktail party once every two months. A group of around twenty of us gather. We each bring something to contribute to the party, either food or drink. She always provides an enticing spread: gourmet pizzas, mini quiches, cheese, and fruit, for example, and our additions just add to the glory. Someone always brings some spectacular homemade dessert like brownies or cupcakes. There's nothing complicated about these cocktail parties. Mostly we just drink wine. There's kettle corn. There are veggies and dip. It's casual, but divine. I look forward to Juliana's Werewolf cocktail parties far more than any fussier event. (Although I do joke with her that I will one day host "high-class Werewolf" where I require a black-tie dress code.)

 Werewolf

So what's all this about Werewolf? you ask. Werewolf is a strategy game with one moderator and a group of players. By picking a card, the players each get assigned an identity (either werewolf or villager) that they must keep secret. The goal is for the villagers to find out who the werewolves are. The goal for the werewolves is to "kill off" the villagers. The players sit in a big circle. The moderator stands. At the beginning of each round the lights go off to indicate that it's night (it's a good idea to play scary music here . . . it helps you get into the mood). Everyone closes their eyes when night falls. Then the moderator instructs the werewolves to open their eyes and pick the villager they would like to "get" (*kill* sounds so vicious). The werewolves select their victim by silently pointing at them. When morning comes (the lights turn back on), everyone opens their eyes. The moderator reveals who was killed. That person is then out of the game, and the villagers have to nominate who out of the group they think is a werewolf. The accused has thirty seconds to defend him- or herself. After this, everyone votes whether or not they think the accused is a werewolf. If they think the person is guilty, they have them killed (again, it sounds so harsh, but while you're playing, it is quite fun). The person then must reveal their card . . . were they a villager or a werewolf? There are other special roles in Werewolf that make the game very fun and varied:

- The Peeker: The peeker gets to peek at night when the werewolves are selecting whom to kill. But if the werewolves catch the peeker opening his or her eyes, they can choose him or her to kill that night. It is very stressful being the peeker, let me tell you.

- The Seer: The seer has the chance to guess who the werewolves are each night, and the moderator tells them if they are right or wrong.

- The Teen Wolf: The teen wolf is a werewolf who must say the word *werewolf* each time day breaks. They must say it loud enough for the moderator to hear them. If they do not say it, they are out of the game.

- The Lovers: The lovers are two villagers who are in love, and if one of them dies, the other dies too.

- The Hunter: If the hunter is killed, they can take out someone with them. If they suspect someone is a werewolf, it's a good idea to choose that person.

If you get the playing cards, you'll see there are many more characters. You can even invent your own.

I realize this may sound completely crazy to you (my husband does not get it at all), but don't knock it until you've tried it. Just picture getting a group of your friends together with good nibbles and cocktails, just letting go, and getting lost in this strategy game that always brings out passion, laughter, and camaraderie. Plus, it just allows you to get silly and not take yourself so seriously. You should see our group. We have writers, actors, film producers, political pundits, and doctors playing this game. No one is too cool, and that's what I love about it. Yes, Juliana's Werewolf cocktail parties are legendary.

Chic Tip

Try combining a cocktail party with a game night. For a smaller group, try a murder mystery evening. For larger groups, try out Werewolf. You will remember it forever. Just don't forget the scary music.

ALBUMS FOR THE EVENING

Beethoven: Piano Sonatas "Moonlight"; "Appassionata"; "Pathétique"; by Vladimir Ashkenazy, Decca, 1984.

Beethoven's most famous sonatas will kick your evening off with dramatic flair.

Petite Fleur by Sidney Bechet, Intense, 2006.

Class up your cocktail hour with this quintessential jazz album.

Chopin: Nocturnes 1–9; Four Scherzi by Arthur Rubinstein, EMI, 2008.

The ultimate classical album to play in the evening to add a bit of drama to your life (the good kind).

Japanese Traditional Koto and Shakuhachi Music by Satomi Saeki Alcvin Takegawa Ramos, Oliver Sudden Productions Inc., 2005.

This traditional Japanese music will inspire you to flow through your evening with tranquil grace.

Kiri Te Kanawa: Ave Maria by Kiri Te Kanawa and the Choir of St. Paul's Cathedral, Philips, 1990.

Play this album after dinner and let Dame Kiri Te Kanawa's rapturous vocals turn your evening into a formal affair.

Adagios for After Hours, Philips: 2000.

Why wait to dream? This tranquil collection of melodies will have you floating on a cloud until your head hits the pillow.

Call of the Mystic by Karunesh, Real Music, 2004.

A fantastic New Age album that will have you chilling after a long day.

ZeNotes by Nadama and Shastro, Malimba Records, 1999.

Calm your mind and get ready for bed with this peaceful Japanese music.

⤳ Dinner ⤳

Breakfast was the opening act, lunch was intermission, and dinner is the grand finale. So whether you are having a light supper or a heavier feast, do your best to make it special. One of the things about my childhood that I greatly appreciate was that every night we ate dinner together as a family. My parents both valued family dinners. The television was turned off. The phone went unanswered. We ate together. It united us, and I can honestly say that it kept me out of trouble as a kid. I was connected to my parents every day for those thirty minutes as we ate dinner and chatted about our day.

Living in Paris as a college student, I saw how Famille Chic took the weeknight family dinner that I was so used to with my family and elevated it to a formal affair. On a daily basis Madame Chic set the table with beautiful linens, cloth napkins, their nice dishes, and a simple centerpiece. Their table manners were impeccable and they placed great emphasis on honoring them. The men seemed to really enjoy allowing the women to be served first. We would wait for the entire table to be served before starting our dinner. We engaged in conversation and listened to music. We enjoyed our meals in courses. Everyone relished the process. Dinner with my French family wasn't stuffy or fussy—they gave it an even deeper meaning with their sense of ritual and adherence to tradition. It is no wonder that I feel very strongly about family dinners.

The table should be cleared of any non-dinner-related items. No homework, no bills, no iPad, and certainly no cell phones. The table doesn't have to be set in a fancy way—whatever works best for you to honor the meal you're having in a convenient way is perfectly fine. You don't have to have a table centerpiece. When you do have one, it will be noticed and feel special.

Making It Work

So the table is set, dinner is ready, and, miraculously, the family actually all sat down at the same time. It's great that you've gotten this far. After this is when it usually spirals out of control. You don't want the food to get cold, so you distribute the plated food as soon as possible. Your family starts to eat, but you're still wandering around the kitchen. You forgot the salt. Oh, and the drinks! You pour the water and get the glasses. Then you realize you also forgot the napkins. Your husband then wants more sauce. The dog is begging at the foot of the table, so you give him his dinner to distract him. Then you finally sit down. Phew. But your family is almost finished with their meal. You feel like you have to eat a little faster to catch up with them. Oh, and the baby's carrots need to be chopped a little smaller. You see where this is all going, don't you? You are wandering around like a servant looking after your family while they enjoy a feast that you prepared. This was my scenario for the longest time, and I'm sure many other mothers can relate. We are so busy taking care of the needs of the entire family that we sacrifice participation in that precious dinnertime we worked so hard to create.

But the thing is, it doesn't have to be this way. Madame Chic certainly wasn't running around the kitchen looking for the pepper while we enjoyed our meal in the dining room. Everything was prepared (I usually helped her) and then we were all called to the table when it was ready and not a moment before.

The key to this is twofold. The first secret is: everything

must be thought out before your family sits down. Everything must be ready. Keep the food on warming plates in the oven, if necessary, but you should not be running around getting everyone napkins after they've all sat down.

The second secret is: you shouldn't have to do all of this by yourself. Have your husband get the drinks. Ask your children to lay out the napkins and silverware. Get the toddler to put the salt and pepper on the table (if they can reach). Feed the dog first if you know his begging is going to bother you. Make sure everything is done. If your family is whining and complaining that they are hungry, explain to them that their food will taste that much better when you sit down as a family the proper way. Tell them that if they help you, dinner will arrive faster. Don't let anyone rush you. Take your time. They will eventually become accustomed to the slight wait. Dinner is the grand finale, after all, and one never rushes a grand finale (even if you are just having fish sticks!).

Chic Tip

. . . .

So you have the whole family sitting together and it's all going pretty well. Now is the time for you to actually enjoy your food. Whatever it is that you've chosen to eat this evening, enjoy it thoroughly. Appreciate it. Delight in it. Celebrate it. Please don't take all the joy out of eating by worrying about calories or fat. Be present. Savor this amazing opportunity you have to sit down with your family, connect, and nourish yourselves.

Making Takeout Chic

In the time I lived with them, I never saw Famille Chic bring takeout home for dinner. Madame Chic cooked dinner at least five nights a week. On the weekends I'd have dinner out with my friends, and the Chics would either be guests at a dinner party or throw their own. Occasionally they'd go to a restaurant. The closest they came to ordering in would be to take some prepared meal out of the freezer and bake it, but that was very rare.

For most of us, however, this simply isn't the reality. Late working hours, afternoon soccer games, and just life in general can get in the way of cooking a homemade meal every evening. Plus, takeout is a big part of our culture. Sometimes you just want that burrito from the Mexican restaurant down the road or the assortment of salads from your local deli on a warm summer's evening.

Just because the meal isn't homemade doesn't mean you can't enjoy it and treat it specially, even on a busy weeknight. Make takeout special by serving the food as you would a precious homemade supper. Use your nice plates. Make the food look attractive. Use your nice silverware and cloth napkins and pour your drinks into glasses. Throw away or recycle all of the paper clutter.

Sometimes the whole family is so hungry and rushed that the takeout containers are left opened on the table. Everyone ends up eating off of the paper plates or out of the container the food came in while plastic bags, forks, and paper napkins are scattered haphazardly around the table. Take pride in your food, no matter what you're eating or where it came from.

Take advantage of the ritual of dining at every opportunity and let no moment go wasted.

⤳ Table Manners ⤲

One of the ways to make your weeknight dinner a formal affair is to observe proper table manners. Pretend you are dining at the Four Seasons and not in your kitchen on a hot summer day. How would you act? How would you expect your family to act? Keep this secret for now. Sit up straight with good posture, eating slowly and enjoying your food. Say please and thank you. After a while your family will just be attracted to the way you eat. If they tend to slump over their food and eat without looking up, rather than asking them not to, just be the change you want to see in them.

It's much more fun to lead by example. When my toddler tries to eat her spaghetti with her hands, I pick up my fork and say, "We eat with our forks." This works so much better than "Don't eat with your hands," which is a negative command and doesn't provide an alternative. Also, I try to say it in a lighthearted way. I try to make it intriguing. *What is all this about eating with a fork?* I want her to think. When she wipes her mouth on her sleeve, I say, "We use our napkins to wipe our mouths," and then I demonstrate. Using positive statements really works well with kids. They won't get it right away, but eventually they will, and there won't be any negative connotations associated with the family meal.

Dinnertime, this marvelous grand finale to your day, is about connection. It is about ritual. It is about tradition. Dinner is about so much more than food. It is a great opportunity to bond with your family and create lasting memories.

Chic Reminders

- Clear the table of any non-dinner-related material. You don't want to dine with any bills, toys, pens, or pencils.

- Set the table as simply or as elaborately as you wish. You can choose to use place mats or tablecloths, candles or a simple arrangement of flowers. You might not have any centerpiece at all. The most important thing is that the table is cleared for the meal. Have the children help you set the table. My older daughter loves to do this. She calls it "decorating" the table, even though she's simply laying down the knives and forks. I like her thinking! It is decorating the table. And doing so, even on a busy weeknight, is treating dinnertime with the respect it deserves.

- Present your food thoughtfully. Even if you are having pizza and carrots, plate it nicely. We often eat what is normally thought of as casual food (our beloved tacos, for example) but it doesn't mean they have to be eaten with sloppy presentation. We will eat them on our nice plates. I'll arrange the tacos (three for my husband, two for me) and decorate them with their toppings so that they look enticing.

- Lead by example and use positive statements to get your family to observe polite table manners. Think of it as a challenge.

- If you want to take your time while eating, do so! Don't let anyone rush you. Enjoy yourself. You worked hard for this.

CANDLES FOR THE EVENING

Twilight onward is the time for soothing, calming, and relaxing scents. These candles can burn long into the evening, providing pleasing aromas that will lull you into tranquil repose.

lavender
eucalyptus/spearmint
pine
sandalwood
vanilla
chamomile
jasmine

⟶ Using Your Best Everyday ⟵

When you love your home and practice being more mindful, you will automatically become more present in your own life. This is living chic. You will want to use your best things on a daily basis. Once you're in the habit of constantly clearing your clutter, you will notice your nicest things more. It suddenly won't seem so absurd to want to use your grandmother's china when you eat your lunch. It won't feel frivolous to give your children cloth napkins to use instead of paper towels. You won't feel overdressed when you wear that pretty silk summer dress to go to the post office. You will notice when other people don't use their best. We will realize that the present moment is all we ever have, so why, oh why would we only use that pretty crystal bowl at Christmastime? Why wouldn't we use it every day to put our fruit in? We see the absurdity that comes from saving our nicest things for later when the pleasure is in the now.

Why don't we use our best on a daily basis? Is it because we're afraid of wearing down our best things? Are we afraid that when a special occasion comes, we won't have anything special to use? Are we afraid of coming across as snobby or unapproachable? Do we think we don't deserve to use the best we have?

The Low-Key Dinner Party

A low-key dinner party can be fun to throw if you keep it simple, are prepared, and have realistic expectations. You aren't going to cook a five-course feast on a Wednesday evening. The point of having a dinner party is not to impress, but to connect with your friends. Once you embrace this idea, you can relax and have fun. Create a warm, intimate gathering where you can discuss the ups and downs of the day, and just life in general. The dinner party should flow into the rhythm of the evening. This will take practice. Using your best dishes and napkins will be second nature to you by now, so it won't be a big deal.

Madame Bohemienne was masterful at throwing the low-key dinner party. She had a busy work schedule and often arrived home in the early evening, but this didn't deter her from entertaining. She would make a simple yet impressive aperitif like the famous champagne cocktail described in *Lessons from Madame Chic*. She would place a few snacks in bowls for us to nibble on as we waited for dinner. Dinner would often be a one-pot meal like *boeuf bourguignon* or coq au vin served with a salad. Dessert would often be her homemade chocolate cake or something as simple as yogurt. Dinner was always served with a fresh baguette, recently purchased from the corner boulangerie. Her meals were simple, yet creative. And despite the fact that she didn't seem at all interested in impressing other people, I was very impressed indeed.

Flourless Chocolate Cake

4 ounces bittersweet chocolate (not unsweetened)

½ cup unsalted butter

¾ cup granulated sugar

3 large eggs

½ cup unsweetened cocoa powder, sifted

Confectioners' sugar for dusting

Preheat oven to 375 degrees F. Grease an 8-inch round baking pan with butter. Line the bottom of the pan with wax paper. Butter the top of the wax paper. Chop the chocolate into small pieces. In a double boiler, melt the chocolate and butter, stirring constantly until smooth. Remove the top of the double boiler and whisk the sugar into the chocolate mixture. Let this cool slightly. Whisk eggs into the mixture. Sift ½ cup cocoa powder over the mixture and whisk until combined. Pour the batter into the pan and bake for around 25 minutes. Let the cake cool in the pan and then invert onto a serving plate. Dust with confectioners' sugar and serve with raspberries.

. . . .

My goal for every dinner party I have is to create a charming and intimate atmosphere. We never have big dinner parties because we live in a small space. We rarely have more than four people over to dinner. Afternoon tea and brunch work for larger gatherings because guests don't need to be seated at a table. We often get visitors from England over for dinner. My husband loves to sit at the table late into the evening, listening to music and laughing about stories from back home. Charming and intimate: a sweet flower arrangement. Thoughtfully chosen music playing. A hearty dish and a salad. Perhaps some dessert purchased down the road at the local bakery. That's all that's needed.

If you are going to be busy the entire day and won't have the time to cook dinner, consider using your slow cooker. Start a dish in the morning, and by the time your guests arrive, you will have a delicious meal ready (can you tell I love my slow cooker?). You'll just need to put together a fresh salad, pour the wine, and warm the bread.

If the day's events have left your home a mess and you feel a bit panicky that guests will be arriving soon, don't worry. Just set your kitchen timer for ten or fifteen minutes (depending on the size of the mess) and get to work. Try to clear and clean as much of the mess as possible. During this time, check your guest bathroom and make sure there are fresh hand towels, plenty of soap, and other necessary supplies like tissues and toilet paper. Wipe down all surfaces and burn a candle in a safe location. Just relax and shake off any jitters. This should be fun!

Chic Tips

- *Husband at his weekly poker game? Invite your girl-friends over for a dinner party. This can be so much fun and a welcome change from girls' night out at a restaurant.*

- *Serve simple, seasonal dishes you are familiar with cooking. Keep it at two courses if you are coming off a very busy day. You can buy dessert. Serve ice cream in old-fashioned ice cream bowls, for example, or have your friends chip in and make it a potluck. The point, again, is to gather and connect, not impress.*

- *Combine casual and elegant—best dishes and napkins but sitting at the card table in front of the fireplace, for example—to make it memorable. On a hot summer night, dine in the garden or on your balcony. Take advantage of every part of your home.*

Trying to Change Other People Is So Not Chic

You might be on a quest to change your life at home, but realize that most people in your family probably won't be on the same path that you are. You must be patient with them and not punish them for not adopting your new techniques right away.

My husband and I are very different people (you know what they say about opposites). He's English and I'm American, so right there we have a lot of cultural differences. We've had many conflicting ideas about life at home, particularly about dinnertime.

I would like to have structured family dinners that are more formal. He would be happy with a more casual arrangement. More specifically, I would like us to eat at the same time every evening, listening to music and talking. He enjoys family dinners but could probably do without them regularly. He also doesn't eat at the same time every day. He is much more of a free spirit than I am.

I would get so frustrated with this. I thought I could change him and convince him that my way was the best way. He agrees that, for the sake of our girls, family time at dinner is very important, so he compromises and sits at the dinner table with us, even if he isn't eating.

I can completely see where he's coming from. He usually isn't hungry when we eat dinner. Sometimes he doesn't eat breakfast or even lunch. Not because it's not available, but because he just doesn't stick to structure or routine. He might catch lunch with a friend or eat at work. If he works through his lunchtime, he doesn't think twice about missing lunch. You can tell already how different we are. I can't believe he doesn't think of lunch as being the intermission of the play!

Anyway, because he often doesn't eat in the morning or early afternoon, he finds himself ravenous in the late afternoon and will eat a large meal or snack at either three or four p.m. Therefore, he often isn't hungry for our early dinner. To many people, especially those who have thoughtfully prepared a healthy dinner for the evening, this would be frustrating. And, yes, I was very frustrated by this. I tried everything to fix this problem. During the day I would send him a text message reminding him about what was for dinner that night, with the hopes that he'd get the hint and eat lunch. Sometimes it worked and sometimes it didn't. I was starting to feel like his mother and not his wife. He's a grown man, after all; he doesn't need me to remind him to eat.

So after countless heated discussions on the subject, I decided to surrender. I can't change my husband. Who am I to say that my way is the right way? Just because it works for me does not mean it works for him. Sometimes he is hungry and eats with us, and sometimes he just sits at the table and has a coffee while we eat. I have learned to accept this. You cannot change other people, only yourself. Does this still bother me? I would be lying if I said it didn't. But I am not willing to turn it into a problem when so much about our home life is actually right.

Also, if I keep persevering with the family dinners, maybe

one day he will embrace them. I just have to carry on with my crusade and be the change I want to see in him.

So if you have a family member who does not do things your way, it's okay. We are all different, and it is their home too, after all. If you accept that it's not your job to change other people—that you only have control over yourself—life becomes a lot easier.

The Arts

As often as you can, take an evening off and seek out the arts. Attend the ballet, visit an art show at your local coffee shop, go see some independent theater, attend a symphony performance or a rock concert. These moments are often too few and far between, especially when family and work life seem to always come first. Indulging in the pleasure of the arts feels decadent and is a magnificent way to recharge your soul. Purchase your tickets in advance. Knowing that you are going to attend the ballet in three weeks gives you something delightful to look forward to.

In one of my favorite Sherlock Holmes stories, "The Red-

Headed League," Sherlock attends a violin concert to clear his head in the middle of working on a difficult case. It is this artistic reprieve that eventually leads him to solving his case. Need to clear your head? Head to the theater, view some paintings, close your eyes and listen to a symphony. Jump out of yourself for a while. The arts put balance and perspective into our lives.

Chic Tips: Arts and the Stay-at-Home Mom
....

It can be very easy to lose your sense of self when you are a stay-at-home mom. Perhaps you had a passion for the arts when you were younger, but now you don't have the time for it. Here are a few ways to include the arts in your life so that you can regularly receive that much-needed dose of culture.

- *Listen to* SymphonyCast *or* The Opera Show *online at Classical KUSC (www.kusc.org). KUSC is a listener-supported radio station that has the most amazing classical music programs. I am a sustaining member and donate a set amount each year to help keep classical music on public radio, but their programs are free and anyone can listen to them. Once you get hooked, you will want to help fund this beautiful resource too.*

- *Have a playdate at a museum. So many museums have free entry, and many have wonderful programs for children. Even if they don't, it is marvelous to walk your ba-*

bies down those marbled halls and look at art together. Get them hooked young.

- *Schedule a night in town to see a play or musical. Go for date night instead of the usual movie and dinner, or take a trip with a group of friends. Planning this in advance and buying tickets can give you something marvelous to look forward to.*

- *If you are an artist or musician, practice your art. Don't give up on it. Make time to paint, play the piano, or sing. Write poetry. Work on that novel. Make time to do what feeds your soul. I wrote* Lessons from Madame Chic *when my first daughter was six months old. If you have a passion and a drive for your art, it can be accomplished.*

⌒⊙ Cleanup Time ⊙⌒

Ah, cleanup time. That oh-so-critical moment of the day when we teach our children to be responsible and pick up after themselves. Certain that I didn't want my daughters to grow up feeling entitled (not to mention clueless) about how to look after their space, I decided to start cleanup time rather young—I'm talking when they were babies. And when they were babies, it was fun to teach them to drop their toy in the basket, but let's get real, I was doing all the work. I was very eager for the time when they'd be older and understand the process.

Well, they definitely got older, and I'm pretty sure they understood the process, but there was one crucial thing they were lacking with regard to cleanup time: ENTHUSI-ASM. Every evening at 5:50, I would chime out, "Cleanup time!" And what was I met with? Not two willing soldiers marching toward the toy brooms, but a scattering of troops. It's like the words *cleanup time* were code for *run!* and then *hide!*

I found myself dealing with this—how shall I say?—*badly* at first. I found myself nagging ("Please! Come on!"), bribing ("If you do this, I'll give you stickers"), and flat-out yelling ("GET OVER HERE NOW"). Uck. Cleanup time had suddenly acquired all of these negative connotations. No wonder they didn't want to do it. I realized I needed them to find the joy in cleanup time. Sure, it's perceived by all (even me) as a mundane task. But isn't that what I get a kick out of? Transforming mundane, everyday tasks into passionate and meaningful activities?

I didn't want my girls to participate in cleanup time because they thought they were going to get something out of it (like stickers), and I certainly didn't want them to do it because they were afraid of Mommy yelling. I wanted them to do it because it brought them joy. So I had to figure out a way to get us to joy.

I came up with a few ideas that I have found work well with the young ones. After all, they deal really well with specifics. A generic wave of the hands and saying, "Please clean up this mess" is not going to get us anywhere. Here are a few chic ideas that I find really work:

- Role-play. Assign the children identities. One can be the chef who puts all the food back in the kitchen set. One can be the conductor who steers the train back into its place. They can pretend to be teachers cleaning up the chalk at the end of the day. Artists putting away their palettes.

- Time yourself. I like to put on one of their favorite songs, which is two minutes thirty seconds long. I say that while the music is on, we put away our toys. We try to put as many away as we can while the music plays. When the song ends, we stop wherever we are and are done. We usually finish before the song ends and just end up dancing.

- Give them one very important task. For example, I'll present them with the empty block bin and tell them it's their very important job to put all the blocks back into the bin and the bin back on the shelf.

- *Can you show me how to do it?* Kids love hearing this and love to show you that they can do it all by themselves. The pride they feel from reminding you that they are "big" kids never gets old for them.

- Give them supplies. Give them child-sized cleaning supplies, like brooms and dustpans. They love to help out and use these things just like Mommy and Daddy.

Family Time

For many families, the evening is the only time everyone can be together. It's nice to mark this daily event with something special and memorable. After dinner, while I'm tidying up the last of the mess in the kitchen, I always put on a few songs for the girls to dance to. The music helps me get through that final push of putting the dishes in the dishwasher and clearing the table. The girls absolutely love this. They dance around the living room shrieking and laughing. I usually finish and join them. Even my husband has been known to break out a few of his moves. Basically, we just get silly. We go with the flow of our mood. If we have a lot of energy, we listen to their current favorite pop song. If we're feeling playful, we listen to the girls' princess music. Dramatic? It's show tunes. If it's a quiet and colder evening, I'll put on classical. We dance to it all. It's a great bonding time for our family. It's blissful.

Nightly after-dinner dancing might not be your cup of tea, but it's nice to find something you can do on a regular basis together: read a passage out of a meaningful book, or sit down and listen to a beautiful song, or tell jokes or ghost stories. Do whatever inspires joy and bonds you together.

Our days are so busy, it can be difficult to plan a meaningful activity to do together every day, but you can also think on a weekly or even monthly basis. Here are some ideas:

- Game night: whenever I visit my parents, we have a ritual of playing the vintage Sherlock Holmes game, 221B Baker Street. (For me, it is pure bliss.) What's your favorite game? You can play it once a month, or to celebrate certain accomplishments.

- Have dress-up night, when you eat dinner in formal attire. It's fun to do this if the kids are going to put on a puppet show or performance after dinner (we used to do this as kids . . . so much fun).

- Let your kids pick a theme. Let's say one night you have to speak in British accents the entire evening (or if you're British, you speak in American accents; you see what I mean). You will all be in fits of giggles, believe me.

- Assume the role of characters from your favorite film and never break out of character the entire evening. Whoever breaks out of character first is out.

It's these silly bonding events that kids remember much later. It's fun to make them regular—the every second Friday of the month, for example—or if you're really into games and role-play, maybe once a week? Do what makes your family happy.

∽ Don't Let the Bedbugs Bite ∽

Ah, nighttime for children is magical. Those little rituals that they are used to: a warm bath, story time, brushing their teeth, combing their hair, and picking out their pajamas, all hold special significance to them and provide great comfort.

It can sometimes be hard, especially after a particularly taxing day, to be patient and go through all of the rituals they love and require. Also, many kids (mine) get that naughty twinkle in their eye around bedtime and might resist the inevitable: actually going to bed. My older daughter is in that phase right now. After cleanup time, I announce that it's bath time. She does various not-so-subtle things to strongly indicate to me that she does not want to take a bath (like completely ignore me, run and hide, laugh, scramble, and scream, to name a few). It is the biggest struggle ever. After a long day, when the only thing getting me through is knowing that I will soon be relaxing on the sofa in my fluffy bathrobe with a cup of tea and a book, my patience (how shall I say this?) would wear extremely thin. I would completely lose my patience with my daughter.

The frustrating thing was, she never wanted to go into the bath, and then once she was in, she never wanted to get out. I would remind her of this every time it happened, hoping she would see the folly in her actions (not so much).

After months of volatile bath times I decided something had to give. I was the adult here. She was only three. I needed to remain calm. I needed to preserve my patience. Instead of running around after her and yelling, I decided to choose calmness. After all, I'm the one talking about cultivating inner peace no matter what happens, right? So why couldn't I practice this with my three-year-old at bath time?

I would get my baby into the bath and sit in the bathroom with her, playing with the bath toys. I would ask my daughter once to come into the bathroom for bath time and that was it. I would not chase her, I wouldn't yell, I wouldn't negotiate. I simply asked with calm authority. Some nights it took a few minutes of her goofing off until she would finally wonder what we were doing and come into the bathroom. After a while, she would come to us immediately. She would surrender and say, "Okay, Mommy."

I cannot tell you how happy I am to have no more (major)

drama at bath time. I couldn't change my daughter's behavior, I could only change mine, and changing mine was the catalyst for her to change hers.

So if you feel as though you are going to completely lose it at the end of the day, chin up. You can do it. Remain present. Remain calm. Conjure up that last bit of energy you have stored in your body to persevere. Bathe your kids, help them brush their teeth, comb their hair, read their favorite book, take turns saying prayers, and tuck them in just so. Nighty-night, sleep tight . . .

Fifteen-Minute Tidy

If you couldn't already tell, I really enjoy timing myself! You've already done cleanup time with the kids, but chances are there is still another layer of tidying that needs to be done so that tomorrow you don't wake up to today's mess. You can accomplish one heck of a lot in fifteen minutes. Set the kitchen timer and get going. If you feel overwhelmed with the mess at the end of the day, set the timer and see how far you get. I bet you will be able to get most of it under control. I also bet if you tell yourself you only have fifteen minutes of work left, you can find the energy to somehow push through.

I first learned about the concept of timing yourself while you tidy from Anthea Turner's *Perfect Housewife* series. In one episode, a woman was complaining that she hated emptying the dishwasher. Who hasn't, at one point in their life, hated emptying the dishwasher? Anthea asked her how long she thought it took to empty the dishwasher. The woman guessed seven minutes. They timed her, and it took less than three. Knowing that it takes less than three minutes to empty the dishwasher makes it seem less awful, doesn't it?

The fifteen-minute tidy has been recommended elsewhere too, most notably by Marla Cilley (the FlyLady) and Emilie Barnes. These ladies are onto the wisdom of timing yourself for fifteen minutes and getting as much cleaning done as you can during this time. I do the fifteen-minute tidy at least once a day. When the kitchen mess looks so unbearable that I can't even fathom tackling it, I set a timer for fifteen minutes and go for it. I can't tell you how many times I have completed my tidy, looked at the timer, and noticed I still had nine minutes left! That means it only took me six minutes to do a job I was absolutely dreading. The fifteen-minute timer puts it all in perspective. With that extra nine minutes I either continue clearing in another room, or I sink into an armchair with a cup of rosehip tea and reflect on the day.

I usually do a fifteen-minute tidy at the end of the day, and during this time I straighten the sofa pillows, put back any stray items that have lost their way, and do any last-minute touch-ups. I almost always finish before the fifteen minutes are up, and, no matter what, I always stop when the timer goes off, even if I haven't finished. I am then free to go off and enjoy the rest of my evening.

Set the Table for Breakfast

At the end of your fifteen-minute tidy, set the table for breakfast the next day. This usually only takes a minute, but you will really appreciate it the following morning when you are still waking up and such things seem like a chore. It is a little luxury to wake up to a set table. I clear the table and wipe it down with my homemade lavender/white vinegar solution and a rag. I lay out the place mats (the children have different ones than we do). I set out the children's water cups and usually put the napkin and silverware down. Get everything you can ready. If you keep the cereal in airtight containers, these can be set on the table. Some people have a lazy Susan that holds napkins and silverware on the center of the breakfast table so the family can help themselves to these items. Now tomorrow when you wake up and go to the breakfast table, you'll feel as though you've been waited on (that is, until you have to make breakfast). If you don't have time to set the table, simply make sure it is clear for tomorrow.

◦ Evening Grooming ◦

Evening grooming sessions can be more detailed than morning ones, as we have more time at night to devote to such things. Do you have any hangnails? Need to wax or thread? Shave your legs? At-home manicure and pedicure? A weekly mask? A deep conditioner for your hair? Give yourself a schedule so you take care of these things regularly and never let yourself go.

Long gone are my bimonthly trips to the salon where I got my nails done. I'm too busy now, and with the added cost of children, I am saving money on certain beauty routines. Because of this I have become a connoisseur of at-home manicures and pedicures. With practice, I have gotten quite skilled at applying the polish, so much so that my nails look professionally done!

DIY Manicure

Using fingernail clippers, trim your nails to the desired length. Using a nail file, file your nails to create rounded or square tips. Be sure to only file in one direction so as not to break the nail. Soak your hands in a warm water/mild soap solution for up to five minutes. If desired, gently push your cuticles down. Apply cuticle oil and massage into fingers. Wipe nails dry with nail polish remover or a nail cleanser (if oil remains on fingernail, the polish will not apply properly). Apply a base coat and wait a moment for it to dry before applying one or two coats of color. Go slow when applying color, aiming to keep it on the nail and not on the skin. If you get nail polish on the skin, you can erase it later with a Q-tip dipped in nail polish remover. Wait for the nail polish to dry. Finally, apply a top coat or gel top coat (Dior makes a great one). Now avoid using your fingers for at least twenty minutes. You don't want to get a pesky chip.

When it comes to nail polish, I find the brands with the thicker brush are easier to apply. A wider brush means fewer strokes to the nail.

Dior's Crème Abricot Fortifying Cream for nails is a creamy salve that promotes nail growth, improves strength, and moisturizes cuticles. It's one of those amazing products that lives up to everything it promises. It's quite sticky, so I like to apply this on my cuticles (on both hands and feet) overnight. In the morning, my cuticles are a non-issue. After using this product regularly once a week, I've seen a marked difference in my nail health and rarely have to push my cuticles back anymore.

Chic Tip

....

To avoid getting polish on your cuticles, apply Aquaphor or Vaseline to the cuticle and skin directly around the nail bed. This prevents the polish from sticking and will give you professional-looking results every time.

DIY Pedicure

Remove any previous nail polish. Trim your toenails short and file in the same direction for smoothness and continuity. Soak your feet in a warm, sudsy foot bath (or simply take your evening bubble bath!). While here, use a pumice stone to smooth out those calluses and heels. Many skin-care systems like the Spa Sonic have a pumice stone attachment that rotates around your foot as you use it. I find this to be extremely helpful in removing calluses and dead skin. After the foot bath, apply cream on your feet and give yourself a small foot rub. Bliss! (Even though you are doing it yourself.) Also apply cuticle oil and push back cuticles if necessary. Then take nail polish remover again and wipe over just the nail to prep it for polish. Apply base coat, two coats of polish, and top coat, waiting for each layer to dry somewhat before applying the next.

Overnight Hair Treatment

Give yourself a luxurious hair treatment while you sleep! Before going to bed, work an oil into your hair and brush it in with a comb several times from the top of the crown to the ends of your hair, making sure the hair is lightly coated. You can use argan oil, coconut oil, olive oil, or avocado oil, all which can be purchased at the health-food store. Once the oil is incorporated into the hair, you can tie it into a loose topknot and place a shower cap over it. If you find it uncomfortable to sleep in a shower cap, let your hair remain down. Just be sure to put a towel on top of your pillowcase so you don't get oil stains on your linens. Sleep in this oil treatment overnight. In the morning, brush out your hair and wash as normal. Your hair will look shiny and feel moisturized.

Exfoliating Body Scrub

Treat yourself to an exfoliating body scrub once a week with this sweet homemade mixture.

½ cup coconut oil
½ cup cane sugar

Mix ingredients together. Rub on your skin while in the shower or bath in circular motions to moisturize and exfoliate the skin.

....

Exfoliating Lip Treatment

When we are dehydrated, our lips can peel and become flaky. Not chic. Mix a dab of your favorite creamy lip balm with a touch of sugar and rub on the lips in a circular fashion to slog off any dead skin. Or use the same coconut oil/sugar treatment described above while exfoliating your body. Wipe away the sugar mixture with a warm, damp washcloth and apply a final coat of lip balm to the lips. Now go drink a tall glass of water.

Chic Tip

. . . .

I often like to take care of several of these beauty routines at the same time. For example, I will put a deep-conditioning hair mask on, as well as a face mask, and do a full-body exfoliation while I'm waiting for the masks to set. Or I will put a face mask on while blow-drying my hair and wash it off before I blow-dry the front sections of my hair. Try to combine treatments to move through your evening more efficiently.

Evening Beauty Routine

Our morning beauty routine was quite simple. We don't want to overcleanse our skin, so we save the real cleanse for the end of the day. Even if you don't wear makeup, now is the time to rid your skin of the impurities of the day like smog, dirt, oils from our hands, and sunscreen. I have several skin-care routines that I follow, depending on the day and how my skin is feeling. Once again, I go with the flow, always checking in with my skin to see what it needs. The following are different ways I take care of my skin in the evening:

- Makeup removal and cleanser: No matter what, I always remove the makeup on my face. I use an eye-makeup remover and then a makeup-removal wipe to take off my foundation. It's important to remove your makeup before you cleanse so that you are not washing the makeup into your pores.

- Cleanser: After makeup removal, I wash my face with a cleanser every evening, no exceptions.

- Exfoliation: I exfoliate the skin on my face and neck three times a week. On the days I exfoliate, I either use an exfoliating brush (like the Clarisonic or Spa Sonic) with a regular cream cleanser, or I use an exfoliant like Epicuren Fine Herbal Facial Scrub applied with my hands (after using a cleanser), or I'll apply an alpha-hydroxy-acid cream after cleansing.

- Oil treatment: Once or twice a week after cleansing (usually on the nights I don't use an exfoliant), I will massage an oil into my face and neck. Yes, you read that correctly . . . an oil! I usually use calendula oil (Éminence has a great one) because of its healing properties, but I love rosehip oil too. I can't tell you how long I have lived with the misconception that oil would make my skin break out. My aesthetician at Petite Spa in Santa Monica told me that oil actually helps to moisturize and heal the skin and won't cause breakouts. You can use a high-quality sweet-almond oil, coconut oil, or even olive oil from your local health-food store. I rub the oil into my skin, let it sit for a minute, then wipe the residue off with a clean washcloth dampened with warm water. Try it; you'll be amazed. Sometimes I combine one or two drops of calendula oil with my night cream and apply on the face and neck. This is another miracle overnight treatment. You'll wake up delighted with how healthy and clear your skin looks.

- Serum and night cream: After these various treatments, I usually apply a serum and then a night cream. With my ring fingers I lightly dab an eye cream underneath and around the sockets of my eyes.

- Mask: Once a week (usually Sunday) I'll apply a mask. My favorite is Epicuren's Volcanic Clay purifying face mask. As you wear it, you feel the impurities being sucked out of your skin. It's simply divine. If my skin feels dry, I'll apply a hydrating mask instead. If I feel it needs healing, I like Benedetta's seaweed mask. If I have any breakouts, I like Éminence's Clear Skin Probiotic Masque. Try out all of those free samples aestheticians and beauty shops give out; find the masks you love that work for your skin.

- Spot treatment: I'm in my early thirties and still get hormonal breakouts, primarily in the chin area. I never thought I'd write that sentence, especially when I was a teenager wishing I was thirty so I wouldn't have to deal with pimples anymore! I'm looking on the bright side: it means my skin is producing abundant oils and looks youthful. Yes, once a month I'll get a spot or two on my chin. So I apply a spot treatment if needed and I move on. Maybe when I'm ninety I won't get them anymore. But then again, who knows?

- Body treatments: Don't forget the skin on the rest of your body! I love luxurious bath products (I mean, who doesn't?) and every day I look forward to using a favorite shower cream or exfoliating body wash. I like to use exfoliating cloths or gloves to get my blood circulating and my skin rejuvenated. I also use exfoliating body brushes. I don't use these things every day, I am a connoisseur of my skin and know what it needs on any given day. Sometimes I just use body wash on a washcloth, sometimes I'll use a body brush, it just depends on what I feel I need.

- Body moisturizer: It's important to moisturize the skin on your body too. I usually use a neutral cream, like Cetaphil, on my legs (they tend to get irritated from shaving). I normally use perfumed body cream on my upper body at night. It's nice to smell good as you drift off to sleep.

While you're engaged in your evening beauty routine, be sure to think beautiful thoughts. Don't obsess about your imperfections—don't focus on your shortcomings. Notice only your beauty. Who cares if you have a few gray hairs. You can cover them up, if you like, the next time you are at the salon. Think about the laugh lines around your eyes as physical evidence of your joy. Don't worry about that pimple on your chin. If it's swollen, put some ice on it and then apply a spot treatment. Don't worry. Breathe. Drink plenty of water. You are beautiful as you are right now.

Chic Tip

....

Believe in aging gracefully. Just look at the messages our society gives us about beauty. When you were a little girl, did you think that once you got older you would automatically become haggard?

Take the story of Tangled. *Rapunzel is kidnapped by Mother Gothel, who basically needs to commit a grand felony in order to remain beautiful. Hmmm. No wonder we have so many beauty and aging complexes! The queen in Snow White? Same deal. Plus you can't open a magazine or go online without seeing ways to combat wrinkles. Women are getting face-lifts, chin lifts, and painful laser treatments, all in an attempt to turn back the clock when it's actually all of this inner turmoil and neurosis that's aging them.*

Sure, it's easy for me to write this right now, as I'm in my thirties. But I tell you what: I am going to keep my good attitude. I'm beautiful and so are you. I don't need some magazine to tell me I need to change in order to be beautiful. If I get wrinkles in my forehead, then I get them. They are a part of me. I will not Botox my face to oblivion and wipe away any traces of emotion for the sake of hiding what is natural. I'm just going to take care of my skin and do what feels right for me. My advice? Do what you want to make yourself feel beautiful. Cover your grays, even get Botox if it's going to make you feel better, but check your inner dialogue. You are beautiful, and don't tell yourself anything else.

Older women have an air of mystery and a mystique about them. They have lived. They have been through it. They are wise. Embrace it. Just love yourself as you are now. Don't panic. It's called life. My mother, who is in her sixties, hasn't had an ounce of work done and she looks absolutely amazing. She barely has any wrinkles because she doesn't stress about her beauty. You go, Mom.

Pleasure

Your day has most likely been packed with watching children, going to the office, and running errands. You must do something for you at the end of the day to reward yourself. Make time to read a book or magazine, take a hot bath, drink a signature drink that you look forward to, watch your special show. Even if doing something for yourself is going to bed at 7:30 p.m., do it! Treat yourself now. You deserve it.

Sometimes if I feel exhausted in the evening, my husband will take over the nighttime duties with the kids while I decompress. I'll usually lock my bedroom door. Then I'll light a candle, run a bubble bath, brush my hair, apply a refreshing face mask, drink lots of water, and soak in the bath for twenty minutes. I might bring a chocolate truffle in and eat it while sitting in my bubble bath. After the bath I'll wander around my room in my pretty pajamas and bathrobe. I'll rearrange the items on my vanity and bedside tables. I'll put all my clothes away and just enjoy how nice my bedroom looks by flickering candlelight. By this time everyone is usually calling for me, so I'll unlock the door, go join in the fun, and then say good night to the girls. It's the small things that bring pure pleasure to an evening like this.

Still Moment

It's nice every evening to have a still moment. This, for me, is right before bedtime. Call it meditation or call it just sitting and closing your eyes while you allow the computer of your body to slowly shut down so you can slide into peaceful sleep. Every evening I say my prayers and then I do a ten-to-fifteen-minute meditation.

When you are meditating, several things will try to infiltrate your mind. You will inevitably think of any problems you have had that day. These problems are coming to you as resistance. They are trying to distract you from sitting still. Even if you're not thinking of problems, you are thinking of your to-do list for tomorrow. Or the bill that you forgot to pay earlier. Send all of these thoughts away. You can acknowledge them, but send them away. Just sit in stillness and breathe. You will notice many sensations. You might get the chills. You might feel light. You might feel grounded. Just notice everything. Observe. Be okay with it. Our minds are running nonstop the entire day, and the voice in our head never really quiets down. You don't have to believe what it says and get worked up by it.

Is this all sounding a bit advanced? Don't fret. I had always been interested in meditation but never had the patience for it. I could not stop my neurotic mind. I thought that I'd have to sit in stillness with a completely empty mind like some Zen master in order to achieve this.

When my husband and I were first married, we decided to take a bak fu pai meditation class at a local yoga center. Apparently my husband and I were the only ones in Santa Monica interested in this meditation at the time, because we were the only ones in the class. Our instructor was so great, one of those magical people. You felt she had a delicious secret she wasn't telling you. Her name was Jennifer too. She was chic in a mystical sort of way. Anyway, the first third of the class we would do yoga stretches and qigong exercises. Then we would sit in meditation. She would lead us into this meditation by giving us a breathing combination and then guide us into the meditation. Okay, this was all a bit strange, but I just went with it. We would sit for around twenty minutes at a time. To a novice meditator this felt excruciating. Twenty whole minutes? Oh my goodness. I'd think about the laundry, the grocery list, a new recipe I wanted to try, my chipped nail polish, the dog, phone calls I needed to make . . . *everything*. I asked her about this, and she said that over time it would get easier and to not force my head to become empty but to just observe the thoughts.

She was right. Over time it became much easier and

very addictive. My husband and I really looked forward to those meditation classes. We never missed one (we felt we couldn't, seeing as how we were the only people in the class). But something changed a few weeks into the course. When we were meditating in the loft, we could hear the loud noises of the people in the café washing dishes and talking below. It really irked me, but I said nothing and hoped it would change by the next class. It didn't. While I was meditating I would hear clanging dishes, laughter, and gossip sessions. It really bothered me. I spoke with the teacher about it, and she said she'd speak to the management. But the next week was equally disruptive. Feeling irked, I sent an email to the owner, asking if her staff would be quieter during the meditation hour. She never got back to me. The next week the noise continued. When the meditation class ended, I also ended my membership with the yoga center and decided to go somewhere else. I was annoyed that the owner never addressed my issue.

Looking back now, I'm not sure if the owner didn't respond to me because she didn't care to or because she didn't feel it was necessary. Maybe she didn't receive my email. Or maybe she knew that one day I would discover that meditation in activity is a thousand times more powerful than meditation in stillness. Being able to have inner peace, no matter what is going on in the outside world, is a tremendous challenge and a tremendous gift. Sure, it was annoying that the people below us were making such a ruckus each week as we meditated, but guess what? Life isn't perfect. It isn't always how we envision it to be. The question is, can we adapt to this while not compromising ourselves?

I find that maintaining meditation in activity gets much easier if you practice meditation in stillness every day. So give it a try. I sit on my bed. I make sure I'm comfortable. You can sit in a chair or on the floor or on the grass in your garden. You can do it under the stars or you can do it when the sun rises. You can do it on the bathroom floor while the kids are banging away at the door, or you can do it in your parked car before you walk into a big job interview. Just sit still, calm your mind, and breathe. Tell yourself that everything is okay, because, guess what? It is. No matter what happens, you are on the right path. Everything is going to be okay.

Remember chic is having inner peace, no matter what. This does not mean we don't stand up for what we believe. This does not mean we don't take action. This means that we walk with purpose through the world, and no matter what obstacles we come across, no matter how exhausted we feel or how wronged we may be, we are able to have inner peace and act with clarity each and every moment of the day. But you can never get here if you don't take the time each day to quiet your mind. To realize the comedy and tragedy of our own thought patterns. To just sit and put things in perspective and to just feel grateful. So try it today. Try sitting in stillness, even if just for a minute. It is the first step toward inner peace.

Winding Down

If you've just come off of your nightly meditation session, it's likely you will feel completely ready for sleep. This is why I meditate right before bed, because it cleanses the mind and always allows me to drift off to a very satisfying slumber.

But there are many other ways to wind down at the end of the night. You could read a book or some poetry. You could have a cup of herbal tea. You could walk around the garden under the starlight or sit on your balcony. Just make sure that you don't stimulate yourself right before bed. If you've ever watched a really action-packed film and then immediately tried to go to bed, you'll know what I mean. Your adrenaline is likely pumping, and you won't feel like sleep even though you are tired. If you do watch an intense film, try meditating for five minutes before you go to sleep. That will help clear your mind and calm your body down.

It's good to limit computer screen time right before bed too. Because before you know it, you'll be checking out the trending topics on Twitter and then getting all riled up over the latest news story or watercooler sensation. And then you'll suddenly find yourself shopping for clothes online. You see the slippery slope.

Do something that gives you joy to wind down. Unplug from the grid. It's time to go to sleep soon. Get excited for your dreams and then slide into that sumptuous bed you made earlier.

ᕯ And So to Bed ᕯ

And so the day is done. You flowed in the rhythm of it beautifully. It probably didn't all go smoothly. I'm sure there were things you'd like to have changed. But the point is, you were present. You showed up. You lived it. And now to bed you go, to recharge not only your body, but your soul. You might revel in exciting action-packed dreams or slumber in quiet solitude. You deserve this rest, and you will need it to get up tomorrow and start again on this glorious journey we are all on called life.

ᕯ The Soul of Your Home ᕯ

A while back I was visiting my parents for a holiday weekend. I went out by myself to pick up some ice cream for the family and took a wrong turn on the way home. I felt lost at first, but then some memory inside me stirred and I remembered where I was, even though my surroundings had changed so much. I soon recognized the entrance to my old neighborhood. While my parents still lived in the same town, they had moved out of the home I'd grown up in, and I hadn't seen it in over fourteen years. Suddenly very curious, I decided to drive through my old neighborhood and go find my childhood home to see what it looked like. The minute I drove through those tree-lined streets, a million emotions flooded through me. So many memories were brought back to me. Riding the bus to kindergarten. Walking to elementary school. The park I played in. The fields I ran though.

As my car approached my childhood home, I didn't miss a beat. I knew the exact streets to turn on, even though I never drove when I lived there. I saw the cul-de-sac I learned to ride my bike on. I remember when we took off the training wheels and my dad gave me a gentle push down the hill. I soared at what felt like rocket speeds all the way into our driveway and crashed into the washing machine in our garage. (It was thrilling.) I saw our former neighbors' houses. I remembered playing in the backyards all day with the neighborhood kids—pretending to be explorers, building makeshift roller coasters, climbing trees.

I finally pulled up in front of our old home. I felt a

tug of pain in my stomach as I saw it had fallen into serious disrepair. While the other homes in the neighborhood
looked just fine, our old home had an overgrown garden
and ripped screens in the windows. I felt a pang of sadness,
as this home was kept in top shape during the time we lived
there. My mother had cultivated such a beautiful garden
out front that people would stop to admire it. And while
we had our ups and downs in this house, in the end it was
a happy place.

Looking at the doorstep, I saw through the disrepair
and remembered so many things that had happened there—
coming home from my first day of school and running to the
door, anxious to get inside. Years later when I was in high
school, my boyfriend walking me to the front door only to
have my dad open it right as we were about to kiss good-bye
(embarrassing!).

Driving to see my childhood home was very significant
for me. It taught me the importance of home, especially to
children. Your home is more than just a shelter. It is more than
just a place to showcase your design skills. It is more than just
a means to an end (especially if you would rather live some-

where else). It is the most important place of your life. It provides you solace and refuge from the harsh world. It provides tangible comforts, like your cozy sofa and warm bed. But it also provides other comforts in the energy it gives off. You will have so many memories in this home. There will be many firsts here, and if you have children, they will remember even the smallest details about your home—especially all of its offbeat character. I felt sad that the new owners of our old home didn't give it the care and attention it deserved. They clearly didn't realize what an important space this home was to our family—what a rich history it had.

But even though our old home had physically seen better days, I knew in that moment that we had taken the soul of that house with us to our new home. And as I had branched out and left our small town, I'd taken all the best bits of home life—the essence of its soul—with me wherever I went. It's the soul that matters the most, after all. And even though over the years I've lived in everything from a cramped dorm room at school to a grand apartment in Paris and finally to our family town home in Santa Monica, I have taken the soul of home with me, wherever I am.

I hope this book inspires you to live your life to its fullest at home. To make every moment special and significant. If you move from your home and drive past it years later, I want you to have good memories—memories that warm your heart and stir up powerful emotions. And about that home you live in now—my wish for you is that you truly thrive in your environment, that you take no moment for granted. That you be chic at home. That you cultivate inner peace no matter what you are doing—whether you're sorting the laundry or doing the dishes, choosing your clothes for the day, or doing cleanup time with your children. My hope is that you choose to be happy and are able find the divine in every moment. You are uniquely qualified to be the connoisseur of your own life. And once you take on this challenge with relish, a sense of humor, and curiosity, you will find your life changing in the most magnificent way. You will carry the valuable essence of a contented home life with you throughout the day. People you meet will wonder what it is about you . . . *Who is that chic person?* they will ask themselves. And you, now in on the secret, will merely smile.

ACKNOWLEDGMENTS

I am very fortunate to have such lovely, supportive people in my life. My deepest gratitude goes out to my family and friends. I love every one of you. Thank you to my agent and dear friend, Erica Silverman, and everyone at Trident Media Group for your stellar guidance. To my wonderful editor/kindred spirit, Trish Todd, and the team at Simon & Schuster for your continued support. To Virginia Johnson for your exquisite artwork. To Nicole Pigeault for your wise words. To Alan Watt for your invaluable mentorship. To the readers and viewers of *The Daily Connoisseur*, who provide me with constant inspiration. To the countries all around the world who have embraced Madame Chic. To Madame Chic herself for continuing to inspire me long after my days in Paris are over. And to Ben, Arabella, and Georgina for being the loves of my life.

ABOUT THE AUTHOR

Jennifer L. Scott is the internationally bestselling author of *Lessons from Madame Chic: 20 Stylish Secrets I Learned While Living in Paris* and creator of the blog *The Daily Connoisseur*. She is a contributing writer for *Huffington Post Style* and has been featured on CNN, the BBC, and CBS News, and in *The New York Times*, *Vanity Fair*, *USA Today*, *Newsweek*, and *The Daily Mail*. She lives with her eccentric husband, adorable daughters, and distinguished Chihuahua in Santa Monica, California. Learn more at www.jenniferlscott.com.